VIP

VIP

Vision Involve Produce

Paul Abrams & Dave Thornton

Cartoons by Ron Tocknell
Diagrams by Stephen Fenton

Douglas McLean Publishing

First published in Great Britain
by Douglas McLean Publishing

ISBN 978-0-946252-89-3

Printed and bound in Great Britain by
Print Academic, Exeter

Cover and typesetting by
Douglas McLean
Set in Adobe Garamond Pro 12/16pt

Douglas McLean Publishing
8 St John Street
Coleford
Gloucestershire
England
GL16 8AR

www.forestbookshop.com/mclean

This Book is dedicated to our families:
Kirsten, Zoë, Corinne, Nic and Tim Abrams
and
Angela, Nat and Essi Thornton

We look forward to you leading us in the decades to come.

Contents

Preface

THE WORLD IS UNLIKELY TO GET LESS COMPLEX IN THE near future and hence the challenge of leadership will grow. Unfortunately, leadership has a mystique it simply does not deserve and this puts off the many who actually lead without recognising it. This excellent book by Paul Abrams and Dave Thornton debunks much of the mythology and should encourage the uninitiated to go forth and lead!

In this easy-to-read book, it feels as if the authors are talking to you, not at you, and there is a great blend of practical stuff with an amazing compendium of contemporary leadership theory brought to life through the vernacular, pictures and cartoons. Paul and Dave have created their own trilogy: VIP, meaning VISION – INVOLVE – PRODUCE rather than Very Important Person. It is helpful to have a new book that extols the simplicities of the fundamental principles of leadership, in the hope that fewer will be daunted, and more will recognise and exercise their 'leadership muscles'.

In commending this book I remind you that it can be read in full on an average train journey but wager that you will dip back into it regularly, such is the wealth of simple and relevant material.

In conclusion, if we want a better world, the size of the leadership challenge is greater than a few individuals with fancy titles can overcome. So sign up to a vision, learn how to involve others and don't just stand there, produce something!

Peter Lees
Founding Director of the Faculty of Medical Leadership
Academy of the Royal Medical Colleges

Introduction

I SUPPOSE THE FIRST THING
WE SHOULD DO IS ELECT A LEADER...

Introduction

THE PROBLEM FOR MOST OF US, EVEN AFTER READING about leadership, is remembering to put into practice what we have learnt.

VIP is a memorable, well-known, world-wide acronym. We hope that by using a simple abbreviation it will remind those who read the book of the three steps of VIP and help them to exploit its messages.

VISION | INVOLVE | PRODUCE

- VISION: The idea and future defined in its full glory
- INVOLVE: Those whom you need on board to achieve that dream
- PRODUCE: The actions that achieve the final product – we considered 'perform' and 'performance', yet at its simplest, leadership produces something, whether that be a product, a concept or a change in attitude or perception.

Let's go forward as we mean to go on . . .

Our **Vision** – To produce a successful, concise book, taking some of the mysteries out of leadership, which assists the reader to develop their own style through insights and practical applications. The bigger dream, of course, is to produce a bestseller, the first leadership book to be transformed into a Hollywood blockbuster, leaving its authors with the Brad/George dilemma as to who portrays whom on the big screen.

To **Involve** you the reader in a very practical sense.This is no academic study but more of a magpie approach to theories and practice that can support leadership development through the simple VIP approach.

To **Produce** – As this book is now in print we've got through the produce phase and hope to inspire you to get on and produce whatever your leadership challenges place in front of you.

The Authors

Dave Thornton works as a successful and sought-after executive coach and 'top team' developer for a range of organisations across the UK. He has worked in a variety of environments and has held a national position within the UK National Health Service. His techniques allow him to deal with the inevitable issues that arise in 'high-performing' senior teams: collisions of egos, hidden agendas and personal ambition to name but a few. He is comfortable with ambiguity, fast-changing agendas, uncertainty and the sometimes inevitable scepticism that can emerge in these circumstances. This is his first venture into print, initiated by the development of a close working relationship with co-author Paul Abrams.

Paul Abrams is Professor of Urology at the University of Bristol and Consultant Urological Surgeon at the Bristol Urological Institute. He has held a number of leadership roles from his student days to the present time, but without realising the power of leadership strategy. He is published extensively in scientific literature but his encounter with Dave Thornton, as a participant on one of Dave's leadership programmes, made him question the basis of the literature on leadership. Being a simple, yet scientific, surgeon he sought the evidence for the leadership dogmas he had read. Dave was not rigid in his attitudes and readily agreed that a straightforward book on leadership that presented a practical approach to leadership, based on common sense, was needed: hence the collaboration to create a Vision, Involve each other and Produce this book.

We hope you enjoy our antidote to the 'leadership lecture'.

Paul Abrams & Dave Thornton

Why Another Book on Leadership?

TO EXPLAIN: WELL, IT'S A CASE OF 'MASTER AND PUPIL', the pupil, naïve and lacking in formal knowledge in the field meets the master, accomplished expert, successful leader and now fluent performer as a leadership coach.

Even though the pupil was naïve, he had had many leadership roles without consciously thinking about leadership. He had had leadership roles such as captain of the school swimming team, and captain of the local hockey club during his training, and subsequently several leadership roles in his profession, all without having given leadership a thought. Then, when very senior in his professional life, he was asked to take on a new leadership role; the organisation suggested he went on a leadership course.

Although knowing you are never too old to learn, it prompted 'Hmmm, at my age? How could I possibly learn anything new? If I'm not a good leader now, I never will be!'

How wrong could he have been?

Wrong enough to be enthused sufficiently to propose this book.

The book reads this way because the authors felt that when you come to a topic from outside, as an older person you seek to simplify the subject. Indeed, when the older of us read an article in *The New York Times* in March 2010 that took time to explain the value of the experienced mature person, who often has the ability to see patterns, that is, to see the 'wood for the trees', we hope that is reflected in our leadership observations.

So, the pupil realised that the principles of leadership are simple and founded on common sense. Although huge volumes have been written on the theories of leadership, it is important to realise that these are theories and not always facts. However, the pupil, as a scientist and doctor, had been brought up to hold theory in one hand and the facts proving the theory in the other. The conclusion from these thought processes were that a book on leadership could be small and concise.

The structure of the book is uncomplicated and it is short and intended to be easily read. We delve succinctly into the theories and works of others whilst adding our own thoughts and comments. We hope the reader will see both the common threads and the overlaps between them and that, especially if you are new to leadership, it enthuses you to explore areas more deeply, no matter how old you are, or your status in life. For the established leader we aspire to prompt some new thoughts and to give useful insights to explore with your protégés.

'This is the Honorary Council of Pretentious Leadership Gurus; The Worshipful Brotherhood of Chartered Accountants is Wednesday night.'

The master inspired the pupil on leadership issues and brings his lifetime's experience, both as a leader and as a coach to many leaders, and gives examples which illustrate some of the issues that leaders have to deal with.

Yet with all these master-and-pupil analogies we hold no ambition to launch a new cult in the leadership genre, no strange mysterious leadership presence lies behind any of this, as in Yoda and Skywalker, in fact the very opposite. So apologies right up front to the geek leadership readers, no conventions where you can dress as the authors will follow this. Sorry, live long and prosper and may the Force be with you.

VIP

Leadership

What is Leadership?

It is not easy to capture what leadership is in a short number of words yet given we are writing this book we thought it important to make an attempt. We would define leadership as:

> *Achieving or changing something by providing energy, inspiration and direction to others, whilst fully understanding and maximising the two-way relationship and the power of mutual respect required between the leader and the follower.*

Leadership is not related to any particular position in society or at work, and leadership can be delivered in any situation, so the assumption that leadership is about holding a dominant position in any hierarchy, we would see as archaic. Similarly, leadership is not simply about your cleverness or your intelligence. As we shall see later, as a leader you may be called upon to lead those who may be cleverer than yourself, and, most alarmingly, your children!

So leadership is about producing something, getting somewhere, surviving something or winning something, yet always with or through the involvement of others hence the following:

VISION – INVOLVE – PRODUCE

Are You a Leader?

As you might have guessed from these comments, many of us are leaders in different aspects of our lives, whether we choose to be or not, recognising that leadership positions can be hugely inspiring for one person and intimidating or overwhelming for the next.

Leadership can occur:

- **At home**, where we may lead the family, either as a parent or perhaps as an older child leading the younger ones, or whilst caring and making decisions for older parents.

  For those readers with children, do you recall that moment when, after the hustle and bustle, joy or trauma of the birth you are suddenly there with a small human, totally dependent on you? Your feelings were probably both inspiring and daunting: conflicting feelings such as this often litter the leadership experience, providing a constant source of motivation.

- **In our social lives**: those of you who have been skiing will know the value of leadership when it comes to deciding which run we should go down, the blue, the red or the black! You may be organiser of the mother and baby group, captain of a sports team or a local hospice charity key fundraiser: all positions or roles that, no matter how great or small bring responsibility to lead others.

- **At work**, we are more likely to have a defined leadership role. This does not always mean that those we lead are answerable to us in job hierarchical terms. We regularly see individuals leading a group of others who have similar jobs and roles. However, we will also explore leadership at all levels, up to the highest, giving Presidents or Prime Ministers as examples of good and maybe not such good leaders.

Leadership Characteristics

Recognised great leaders Nelson Mandela and Mahatma Gandhi were characterised by their charisma and presence. However, this was achieved through calmness, dignity, total honesty and even quietness. This contrasts with others, who would be termed as effective leaders, whose demeanours were quite different, using humour and the ability to communicate with ordinary people as major positive characteristics. For example, some might nominate Ronald Reagan or Diana, Princess of Wales, or even the attempts of Vladimir Putin. Of course, all kinds of other factors are at play that affect our bias towards one or other person as a leader. Some people from the world of popular entertainment have become influential beyond their particular acclaimed talent, to become ambassadors for particular causes, such as Bob Geldof with Live Aid.

Be cautious, though, don't cross the line between influential leaders with impact, or just well-known personalities with views and large egos. In a tabloid headline-grabbing world, many may confuse the two, as one traditional view of the Leader is the big speaker, loud, brash and inspirational, leading from the front, or preaching from the podium.

We must not forget those who lead by their sheer determination and actions or stance against overwhelming odds: in politics there is Aung San Suu Kyi, the long-standing Burmese civil rights campaigner, and in exploration Ernest Shackleton, who famously never lost a man in conditions where most would have perished.

So, you can see, there is no blueprint for the characteristics of a leader and much has been written about leadership, with many theories in existence. Our role here is not to reopen or prolong debates about whether leaders are born or evolve.

Instead, we would capture some clear, positive characteristics that we believe are commonly found in good leaders, including:

- Courage – to speak out and act on their beliefs and vision
- Resilience – not only to survive challenges but to thrive
- Value-driven – the ability to live out the values they espouse, for all to see
- Futurists – the ability to see beyond what is now, to what might be
- Tolerant – riding and understanding the ups and downs of leading others
- Listener – to others, even those whose message is hard to receive

- Truth-giver – the integrity to give truths, good or difficult, with positive intention

All these characteristics are best accompanied by enthusiasm, commitment, optimism and of course no significant or obvious irritating features. Is all this beyond you? Can any one person really encapsulate all these things? Being a good leader is no easy task and a good helping of humility along the way is a real strength. So any current questioning of your own ability we will excuse temporarily as your own humility leaking out.

Rob Goffee and Gareth Jones are two leading experts on organisational culture and leadership, and have studied many leaders in change in detail. They make the seemingly obvious statements that leaders must:

- Be inspirational, caring about what they do and what they want those following them to do
- Have vision that leads to clear strategic direction
- Have energy
- Have authority through their intellectual and practical abilities

Steve Radcliffe, one-time marketing director and chief executive, has spent the past 20 years helping to develop leadership and leaders. He has developed ideas of energy in leadership, arguing that energy is of one of the fundamental essentials of leadership and has to be managed by the leader, and also in those around him or her.

Four types of energy are described by Radcliffe in his book, *Future-Engage-Deliver* (Troubador, 2008):

i) Intellectual energy: this is essential to the critical thought processes needed at every stage of VIP

ii) Emotional energy: is the energy you use in your interactions with others. A good leader shows emotional energy in a positive sense to bind others together. Yet a leader should not be afraid to show genuine negative emotion, such as annoyance or even moderate anger, should the occasional situation warrant this.

The leader's positive emotional energy is what can often prove infectious, and stimulating to those around them. Emotional energy is essential to show you care about your VISION and as you INVOLVE those around as you.

iii) Spirit energy: this is the energy that provides your inspirational qualities and drives your vision in particular; it taps into something deep and fundamental to the leader's beliefs and values.

iv) Physical energy: this seems to come naturally to most effective leaders who manage consistently to maintain their physical state by eating reasonably, staying fit enough and sleeping an adequate number of hours, in order to maintain their intellectual, emotional and spiritual energy to lead.

Interestingly, Goffee and Jones came up with four further characteristics that we might not immediately think of. Try to think about these in relation to yourself:

i) Leaders admit to their weaknesses: they explain that weaknesses make the leader human and, providing the weaknesses are not fundamental flaws, such as a financial leader not being numerate, then admitting one's weaknesses can only be beneficial, and enables the leader to do something about it, or ensure someone else does on their behalf.

QUESTION – What are your weaknesses, and to whom can you express them, in order to address them; how comfortable is it for you openly to express a weakness?

ii) Leaders are intuitive: they can sense when a different approach or action is needed. They can sense when and why something is going well or badly, and know what to do to reverse or encourage the process.

QUESTION – How sensitive are you to changing circumstances around you? How often are you looking up, out and beyond the immediate?

iii) Leader use 'tough empathy': what Goffee and Jones mean by that is that the leaders care about what they do and those who are working with them. However, they are realistic and able to be decisive and take tough decisions with and about those around them when the circumstances demand this.

QUESTION – How do you display that you care about what you do and about those around you who help or assist you in doing it? Is it open, expressed and articulated, or left for others to 'just know'?

iv) They dare to be different: this may be a physical, an emotional or an intellectual difference. Often leaders are unaware of how different they are from those around them. However, if they understand these differences, they can utilise them to make their leadership even more effective.

QUESTION – what is different about you? What will people remember? Don't let difference hold you back: embrace it, promote it, work with it as part of what it makes you. One of the authors has a strong northern English accent and was constantly told to change it, indeed memorably once to 'lose it'; instead he embraced it, not to the extent that he exaggerated or played on it, just accepted it was part of who he is and now speaks on many stages with confidence. And you know what, people remember him.

This leads to a fundamental truth in leadership. Leadership is about honesty, and honesty is about what and who you are. It is not a game, not play acting or pretending to be the leader, turning it on and off when needed. It is probably true that people can fake the good leader in the short term, turning on the charm, saying the right things and speaking to the right people. Yet truly good leaders are true to themselves, still open to change and development, and constantly challenging themselves to adapt and improve over the long term.

The more comfortable a leader is with themselves, the more genuine they come across, the more competent they are to lead, and if there are slight defects or quirks that are unique to them, they are forgiven and excused with those defects even becoming endearing qualities.

Leadership and Management

IT IS IMPORTANT THAT WE HAVE A DISCUSSION ABOUT leadership and management and try to understand what the differences are, so that when we have to lead we lead, and when we need to manage we do just that. We can start with the derivations of the two words.

- **Leadership.** The word 'lead', in the context of leadership, derives from the North Germanic *laithjan,* which was derived from *laitho*, meaning way or journey, from which comes the English word 'load'. Etymologically then 'to lead' means 'cause to go along one's way.' 'Ship' as a suffix comes from Old English as in froendscipe (friendship)

- **Manager** comes from the Italian word *maneggiare*, 'to train horses', which in turn derives from their word *mano,* meaning 'hand'. This was the word used for the men who were responsible for handling the horses and the carts that supplied everything that the

> fighting Roman soldiers needed. These men provide the wherewithal that allowed the expansion of the Roman Empire, by ensuring that all the resources and backup were in place to allow the task to be undertaken.

These definitions lead us to ask two questions:

- Do leaders manage?
- Do managers lead?

This book is about leadership and hence presumes that leaders will spend less time undertaking a management role. Hence one answer to the question is that, ideally, leaders do not manage and therefore managers do not lead.

If only it was that simple.

Some people have written that they believe that separating the two is unhelpful. Henry Mintzberg in *Debunking Managements Myths* stated:

> 'My view is that management without leadership is disheartening or discouraging, and leadership without management is disconnected, because if you lead without managing, you don't know what's going on. It's management that connects you to what's going on. We can make the distinction between leadership and management conceptually, but in practice I don't think we should.'

We would agree that both are essential, yet when it comes to personal development understanding the difference is crucial. To enhance your personal impact and success, where is it you need to place your attention, improved management abilities or leadership abilities? There are many good managers whose working knowledge of systems and tools are excellent yet they couldn't inspire themselves, let alone anyone else. There are others whose inspirational quotes flow effortlessly arousing emotion, inspiring commitment, pumping up the energy levels, then proceeding slowly to deflate everyone around them by not having the ability to follow through with actions or to deliver on promises.

For many people the movement from manager to leader is a natural progression as their career develops, and therefore knowledge of the differences, and where to put their development effort, becomes increasingly important in order to triumph in their particular field or business.

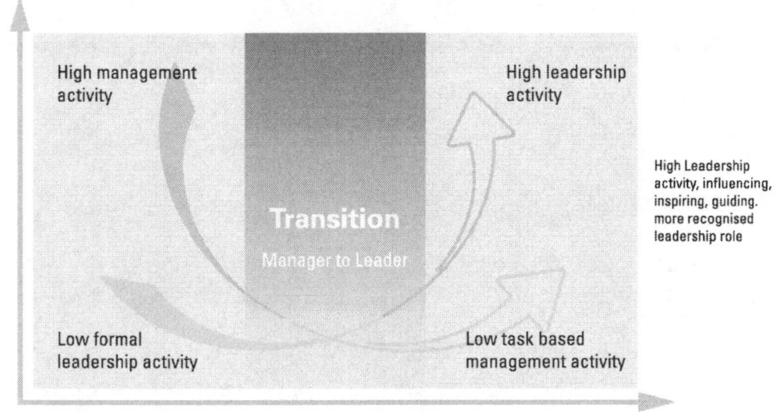

At every moment, it is important to know whether you are in a leadership role or whether you are in a management role. The role of managers and management is to provide the facilities and resources for the leaders effectively to carry out VIP.

Many people in large or complex organisations start their

careers in very transactional roles and as they progress, their role becomes more strategic, bigger, and with communities of people to inspire and enthuse. Becoming an effective leader is often dependent on a person's ability to reduce one set of behaviours and develop another, quite different set, as they make that transition from manager to leader.

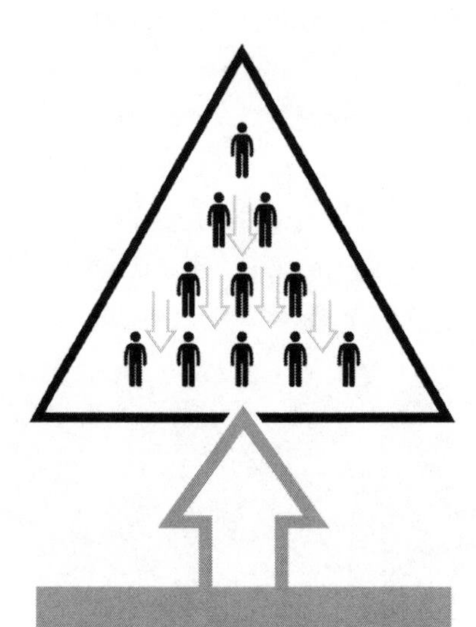

Hierarchical structures exist in many organisations. At its strictest this model establishes authority in a downward chain of command, which is difficult if not impossible to challenge or question. For some organisations and tasks this may be considered essential.

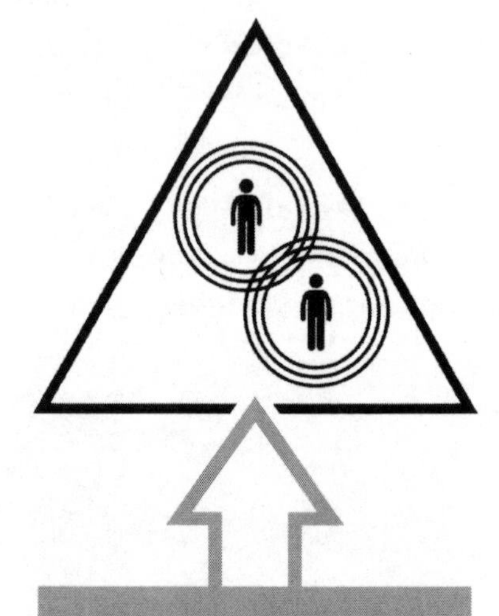

Other organisations may define or encourage leadership at all levels. Where anyone can influence change or improve performance, regardless of their status within the structure. Yet it is usual that some hierarchical chains of command and decision making structure are still required.

Management or Leadership

We often hear management referred to as 'managing up', as in 'I need to manage my boss', or 'managing down', as in 'I need to manage those who report to me.' This very two-dimensional view relates more to a hierarchical management structure than to leadership.

Effective leaders can emerge from anywhere, causing leadership ripples that send echo soundings out around them, providing energy, clarity and enthusiasm. Good leaders resonate, and their resonance often extends beyond the boundaries or confines of their immediate environment and even beyond organisational limits.

Here we would invite you, the reader, to recognise leaders around you. Not because of their designated position, but because of who they influence, and how they achieve things: you know of their presence and their achievements. We would then further ask, if you are their senior, are you prepared to nurture their presence and leadership potential or are you threatened by it?

There is much written about succession planning and leadership development. Good leaders by definition breed good leaders. Sadly, too many of us know the pseudo-leader who enjoys the 'boss' role, and who crushes those whom he or she feels are getting too near his or her status, stature or levels of influence, in order to maintain and protect their own sense of identity and power.

What sort of leader and person are you?

As we've said, there is no blueprint or standard Identikit leader. Leadership has been studied and commented on since the early Greek civilisation, so if there was a surefire winning

'I must say Henry, listening to all these diverse views of the world is thoroughly exhilarating.'

formula or personality type, surely we would have nailed it by now and probably exploited it, certainly in a military or sporting arena. Perhaps in the future we will identify that specific leadership DNA and clone leaders to run the world. We think not.

Leaders have a wide variety of characteristics and reflect the wonderful diversity that is humankind. These could be termed personality types or just differences in who and how we are. So, at least in some part, the type of leader you are is determined by the sort of person you are.

Understanding Yourself and Others

ANOTHER ESSENTIAL ATTRIBUTE OF A LEADER IS THE ability to understand those around him or her and not to make the assumption that individuals will think, feel or behave in the same way that he or she would. This is a very common and natural mistake. As we go on to discuss different people's preferences, it becomes easier to understand, and at times even predict the way others may perhaps think, feel and behave.

We have conducted a number of leadership courses, and it is interesting to note that some attendees would arrive five, ten or even thirty minutes late for the session. This allowed us to ask the interesting question as to how leadership and timeliness are associated. This could perhaps be paraphrased as 'leading by example'. One CEO advocated repeatedly the importance of timely interventions for the customer, 'Right people, right place, on time' was a common mantra he espoused; yet he himself often arrived late or on occasion

'. . . I'm on my way as we speak . . . stuck in traffic . . .'

'. . . Sorry I'm late . . .

Wrong time, wrong place

even at the wrong location. Although always apologetic with detailed explanations of why he had kept others waiting, the incongruity with his own mantra made those around him doubt his leadership qualities and question his motives (as well as considering him a complete prat.)

Effective leaders know about themselves, their strengths, their motives and their potential blind spots. Knowing all this is in itself a considerable strength, yet how accurately do you know about yourself? We can at times have a tendency to believe what we like about ourselves and seek selective evidence to support that particular image.

Coaching the most experienced of people, it is still astonishing to notice how we can get the perception of ourselves so amazingly wrong. One senior leader described brilliantly how he engaged, persuaded and encouraged others. Amazed and delighted by his description of his own performance, we sought to explore his style further, through talking to those who worked around him. We did this in the hope that we might better understand the subtleties of just how he influenced others, so that we could subsequently share these insights with those wanting to expand their leadership qualities. Wow, what an insight we gained into him, by asking others. He used 'persuasion' techniques that most would refer to as covert threats, and 'encouragement' that focused on the adverse consequences of not doing as he wished. Could they really be talking about the same person we were coaching? Oh yes they were.

The opposite can be found in leaders who say they lack confidence and describe how they struggle to motivate and persuade others, and have the belief that others may see them weak or indecisive, only then to find out their colleagues find them inspirational and supportive, and as a consequence give them real loyalty.

These misconceptions of ourselves should be no surprise. It happens to most of us on the subject of age; ask one of us (the authors) how old we are and we will give you our chronological age according to our birth date. Ask us how old we think we are, and we will shave off 10, even 15 or 20 years: our perception changes. Who do you know who thinks they are stunningly attractive to all others, and is not, or believes they could pack out any global stadium with their amazing vocal talents, and could not? So understanding yourself, including your good, bad and indifferent qualities, is an important hallmark of the leader and essential if you are to play to your strengths, and compensate for your lesser qualities.

So how do you discover what kind of leader you are?

- **One to One** – Structured discussions with those who work closely with you and around you, including your peers, those to whom you report, and those who report to you. If brave, you would also include those who may not sing your praises, or who may even have been openly critical of your style and approach in the past. It will take some preparation, teeing up the conversations by preparing them as to what to expect, giving them permission to be honest and reassuring them that the information you get from the exercise will be used for everyone's benefit. It is important to give the discussions a focus and concentrate on some specific areas in the expectation of getting them right. Open-ended conversations without structure can be too wide-ranging and ultimately confusing or contradictory.

- **360 feedback** includes various methods of receiving collated feedback from all those who work around you, from paper-based questionnaires to complex online tools. This extremely beneficial and insightful approach can give clear indications into just how you are perceived and performing as a leader.

  We do feel the need to point out the danger of a blanket 360s approach, 'Let's all do a 360'. This is a sharp tool and therefore can be misused and damaging. People need to be in a reasonable state of mind to get full benefit, and respond positively to its findings. Even though usually anonymised, the human mind is inquisitive and needs to resolve unknowns. So much effort can be focused on 'I wonder who said that' or 'scored me that', rather than taking on board the real message. It is rather like the office 'Secret Santa' where anonymised individuals draw names from the hat and secretly buy a seasonal gift for the name they draw. The whole process usually ends up with all the effort going into trying to work out who sent you the gift (because that will affect your judgement of how much you like it or not) and detracts from just appreciating the gift – 360s can be just the same but less fun.

- **Read** about leadership and management: do you recognise the qualities you are reading about in yourself, do the insights indicate that you have further development needs you must embrace?

- **Dual Coaching** – Coaching has traditionally been a one-to-one relationship between a coach and a coachee, focusing on enabling the coachee to achieve their goals. But what if the need for coaching is to enable a business partnership to work more effectively? Dual coaching saves vital time and resources and can prove an effective approach to boosting the performance of two people who work together in leadership positions. Giving joint clarity and a shared, solid understanding of business direction and priorities, and most importantly, providing new insights that ensure differences are strengths to be built upon and celebrated, and are not cracks for others to exploit.

- **Reflective Mentoring** – Stop and think, step back and just take a look at what you are achieving, giving focus to a number of priorities. By taking time to stop and give some serious reflection you can ask yourself some big questions and face up to the reality that you should be experiencing.
    - Can you articulate your vision?
    - Are you achieving progress with your VISION?
    - Do you have loyalty from those around you – and how do you know?
    - Is the team around you happy?
    - Can you demonstrate regularly listening and responding to others?
    - Is what you are doing successful – and by what/ whose measure?
    - Are your business goals being met?

- What courageous things have you undertaken?

These questions and many more should be considered in good reflection time. Some people make natural reflectors and may look back regularly at what they have undertaken in their leadership role; others may need to learn the discipline of good qualitative reflection. Not to do so could lead to more 'blind spots' and greater misconception about ability. The other side of the coin, for those who overly reflect, is that it should be a productive process and not one of anguish or self-flagellation.

So when the leader understands him or herself the challenge then begins of understanding others.

There is no one global accepted definition of personality types, just lots of theories, some helpful, many not. We're going to refer briefly to three ways of looking at different types of people and their preferences: you are likely to feel that one or more of these methods are easier for you to relate to. You may also find these methods useful when you are leading others, when you want to anticipate how they will react in the VIP process, and how you might alter your approach to that individual, and understand what 'makes them tick'. We choose these three because of their simplicity and in the belief that each gives different insights into yourself and others, and this knowledge and awareness can strengthen a leader's ability to lead.

We shall briefly cover:

1. **Merrill and Reid's concept of preference**
   Defined by Ask/Tell, and Show emotions/Don't show emotions.

This gives a simple way of understanding how people work differently and how they are perceived by others. It is a simple quadrant structure which is easy to understand and apply in the workplace.

2. **Baddeley and James' Political Awareness**
   The four types are defined by political awareness, to political naivety, and psychological game-playing, through to acting with absolute integrity. This gives an insight into working within the 'political' environments that many of us face, from government and national politics down to office politics and handling relationships.

3. **The three-ego concept, within Transactional Analysis (TA), covering the child/parent/adult.**
   This gives great information about relationships and how we react to various individuals and situations in different ways. Although much has been written on this complex area, knowing a little of some of the basic concepts can give an insight into what might be going on in any situation.

There is a warning attached to this section.

We include this section to help consider differences and not to confirm what you are or are not, as many people who have undertaken personality type tests then adopt the results, to explain away their weaknesses, or excuse something which they have not undertaken to an adequate standard. Many companies can invest heavily in development packages that essentially just categorise people through discovering their preferred ways of working or weaknesses, yet without the appropriate subsequent personal development programme. This approach can actually reinforce negative issues rather than redress them and inadvertently affirm and cement perceived weaknesses, placing people firmly in a stereotype. 'As the accountant I don't do vision, just detail' or 'being an introvert, I'm far too quiet to lead from the front' . . . nonsense.

Having read about the three different models of identifying and describing preferences (differences) we have used, don't worry if you are attracted by different parts of all three. You as an individual are likely to have elements of different preferences in whichever approach or theory you look at.

Indeed, it is probably healthy that we use a mixture of preferences, as this may allow us to deal more effectively with the leadership issues we will face.

We introduce this section to explore the differences between us, and to acknowledge that successful leaders recognise these differences and are able to adjust their approach to enthuse and engage with those who are not 'like them'. Indeed many studies have pointed out, that when organisations go 'wrong', they go wrong due to 'group think' and due to too much similarity in thinking. Diversity is good, it's great that all these differences surround you. You may not always think that, when the irritating guy from B section is rattling on, yet again, about the need for more detailed analysis: consider that you might actually need him, go on, admit the possibility! Or, when one of your direct reports insists that you 'paint the bigger picture' for others to better understand where you are heading: she may well be right. Good leaders recognise and embrace differences, utilise them

'Once again Paul's preference became obvious to all (except him)'

to their full potential, and avoid them becoming a point of friction.

When recalling one of our own experiences where someone very different from us was, from our perspective, 'ranting on again', we spent far too long at loggerheads, focusing on the physical process of ranting. It was only the deepening of understanding of our differences that allowed us both to not only make allowance for those differences, and therefore become less irritated by each other, but to go on to make best use of the differences, noticing how discussions that were once tense and uncomfortable, swiftly became challenging yet creative, even fun and something to look forward to. Both of us recognised the advantage and even the huge benefits to each other and the business at hand.

Merrill and Reid's Concept of Preference

Merrill and Reid developed their preferred working style types by looking at two factors.

Ask or tell, and control emotion or show emotion.

This is about preference and is not saying that one preference is better than another; there are as many good as bad ways to ask, as there are in how you tell people things. Likewise it makes no judgment on those who do or do not express emotion.

People who
CONTROL EMOTION

Analytical	**Driven**
• Formal • Measured/systematic • Seeks accuracy/precision • Dislikes unpreparedness / surprises • Wants to know HOW	• Business-like • Fast and decisive • Seeks control • Dislikes inefficiency • Wants to knowWHAT
Amiable	**Expressive**
• Confirming • Less rushed / more easy-going • Seeks appreciation • Dislikes insensitivity / impatience • Wants to know WHY	• Flamboyant • Fast and spontaneous • Seeks recognition • Dislikes boredom / routine • Wants to know WHO

People who
SHOW EMOTION

Think how each of these types could contribute best to the VIP approach:

- EXPRESSIVES may provide much-needed energy and optimism, keeping the vision alive and even fundraising or delivering publicity.

- AMIABLES may well ensure the team works well together through fostering relationships and ensuring that there is a common understanding as to why the task is being undertaken.

- ANALYTICALS may define best how the task will be done or what information is needed, and their ability to critique could prove essential when risk assessing.

- DRIVERS can ensure the product is completed on schedule, and to cost, without becoming distracted by peripheral issues.

While working with people we notice that although they often claim to be able to move to each of these identified quadrants as necessary, with further exploration, they usually identify two with which they are more comfortable. To increase our awareness, it is important to understand how others may perceive the various preferred styles we adopt, both positively and negatively.

Other perceptions of the different types are:

The Expressive: The Social Specialist

Perceived positively as:	Perceived negatively as:
Verbal	A Talker
Inspiring	Overly dramatic
Ambitious	Impulsive
Enthusiastic	Undisciplined
Energetic	Excitable
Confident	Egotistical
Friendly	Flaky
Influential	Manipulating

The Amiable: The Relationship Specialist

Perceived positively as:	Perceived negatively as:
Patient	Hesitant
Respectful	Wishy-washy
Willing	Pliant
Agreeable	Conforming
Dependable	Dependent
Concerned	Unsure
Relaxed	Laidback
Organised	Organised
Mature	
Empathetic	

The Driver: The Command Specialist

Perceived positively as:	Perceived negatively as:
Decisive	Pushy
Independent	One man/woman show
Practical	Tough
Determined	Demanding
Efficient	Dominating
Assertive	An agitator
A risk taker	Cuts corners
Direct	Insensitive
A problem solver	

The Analytical: Technical Specialist

Perceived positively as:	Perceived negatively as:
Accurate	Critical
Exacting	Picky
Conscientious	Moralistic
Serious	Stuffy
Persistent	Stubborn
Organised	Indecisive
Deliberate	
Cautious	

In extreme stress situations, these individuals can move diagonally to the opposite corners.

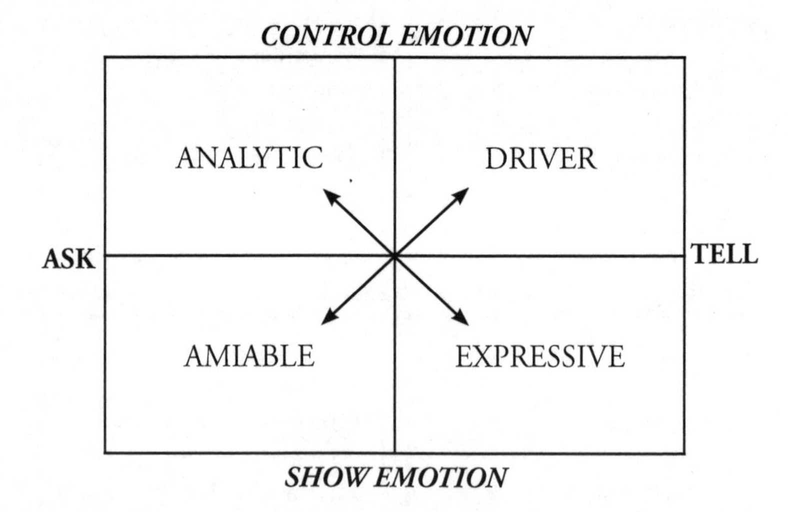

We would invite you to consider just yourself when there are high levels of stress and to see if you recognise these reactions in yourself or in others around you.

- Analytics become aggressive, sarcastic and even offensive and move towards being Expressive. 'I told you it wouldn't work', or 'you were determined to rush, I could have predicted that'.

- Amiable people become autocratic and move towards becoming a Driver: 'enough's enough', or 'it's time something was done about the . . .'

- Drivers become more extreme and then may even seek allies with 'quasi-amiable' behaviour and are then likely to disrupt the team, 'I'm not happy with this and I know my colleagues share this view'.

- Expressives can withdraw and become more like Analytics! The thing is, because they are Expressives everyone will know they have withdrawn. They may also react by suddenly requesting detailed information, in order to slow down or even block movement.

The Expressive quietly withdraws from proceedings.

BADDELEY AND JAMES' POLITICAL AWARENESS
Which political animal are you?

Baddeley and James, asked 'What political animal are you?' and developed two different spectrums on a scale from:

- Extreme 'Psychological game-playing' through to 'Acting with (absolute) integrity', and
- Very 'Politically aware' through to being totally 'Politically unaware'

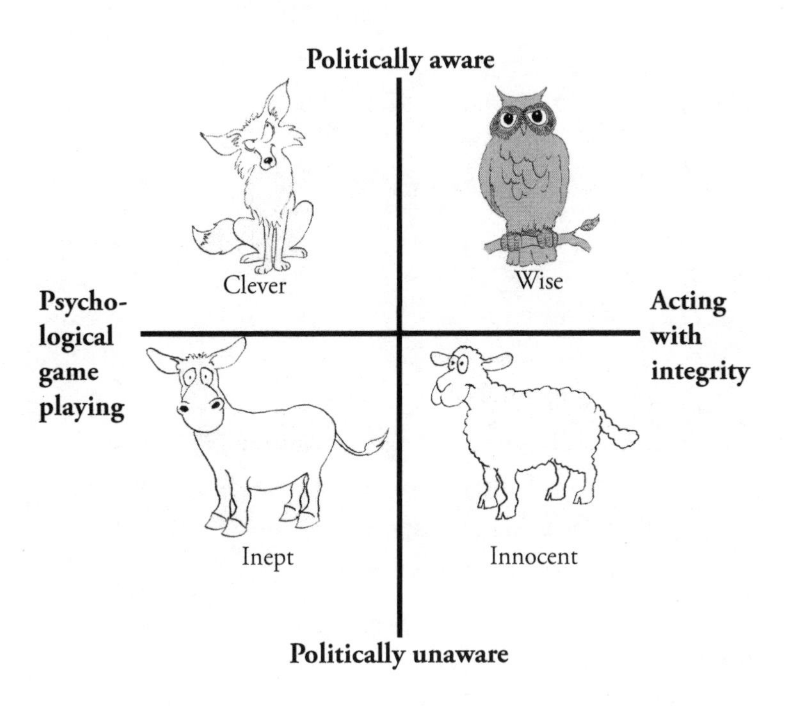

Typical features at the extreme of these quadrants include:

At the extreme, Donkeys:

- like to associate with authority
- use clichés and jargon
- pursue their own interests
- could be prone to social gaffes
- play the wrong hand at the wrong time
- try to network, but unsuccessfully

At the extreme, Sheep:

- trust indiscriminately (especially authority)
- stick to the rules
- respect expert and positional power
- are loyal and ethical
- fail to network or see its value

At the extreme, Foxes:

- pursue only selfish interests
- are like chess players using people as pawns
- are charming but incongruent
- know (and use) the formal and informal networks
- can be calculating: encouraging others' disclosure but rarely disclosing themselves
- seek and wield power for own success: 'the game is all'

At the extreme, Owls:

- have clarity of outcome
- are interpersonally skilled and value-driven
- use power not only for their own interests, but for those of others

- act with openness, honesty and loyalty
- actively use informal/formal networks and procedures
- seek common ground

'Our preferred types aren't always easy to hide from others'

Whenever we have included this in any aspect of our development programmes, sure enough a strange thing happens; people in the room grow wings, their eyes expand and they are prepared to work into the late evening as they prefer the dark!

So, stop, and re-read the extreme points from each quadrant, you have never done any of these?

No, no, don't read on, STOP!

If you are going to get anything from this book and indeed develop as a leader, being honest with yourself is a pretty healthy place to start.

No doubt, we have all displayed many of these behaviours ourselves, and probably continue to do so, depending on the circumstances and context in which we are operating.

Baddeley and James' four animals prompt other insights and comment from us, so expanding on this we would ask, could it be that . . .

The donkey is inept and gets put upon, taken advantage of, 'the beast of burden', and is even being used to do others' (fox) unpleasant deeds. Their desire to get on and influence, without any political awareness, constantly works against them, although they have little insight and don't notice this. How often have you realised, far too late in the day that you are or were behaving as the Donkey? They are also clumsily plodding along thinking they are being smart, ever clever with their political moves, yet everyone around can see exactly what they are up to, and often have a good laugh at their expense.

The lamb is innocent and naïve, perhaps at times afraid: 'lamb to the slaughter' could well be appropriate. If the lamb is too naive, they could become vulnerable to the exploits of others. Yet there are times we may use naivety or vulnerability to gain strength, admitting our weakness or lack of knowledge in order to gain more. Classically in a new post or role, asking the apparently stupid question is excused, and can be very useful. Lambs don't make obvious leaders, their naivety gets in the way and they are prey to the clever fox, who will outmanoeuvre them every time.

It is important not to forget that in large organisations

and workforces many people want to take the lamb role, even choose it, not wanting to become embroiled in the politics of the world or the organisation, but arrive, take instruction and enjoy the job they enlisted to do. We are dependent on lambs and should look after them and lead them well.

The fox is clever and may be regarded as scheming. If too far to the upper left, then the fox will not be trusted, and trust is important for the leader to succeed in VIP. Yet when the pace and scale of the challenge is on the up, and all those personalities working around you are doing whatever they do, good and bad, how often do you treat one differently to another or disclose information or motives differently to one than another? When threatened, especially at times of change, is it human nature to look after yourself first, before everyone else? Ah, the owl now appears to be growing a short brushy tail.

The owl: Everyone wants to be the owl. However, if the owl moves too far upwards to the right, is it possible that they can't move because they have taken the moral high ground and are so morally driven that they fly too high and become aloof and detached from reality? So, is it possible that they then become obstacles to change, as their ability to compromise or find creative alternatives is diminished and becomes almost impossible? You will ultimately decide where you wish to be, but many would wish to be in the middle and well above the horizontal line towards political awareness. It is certainly true that to be successful in leadership, having political astuteness, and operating with a particular political savvy is imperative. Understanding politics and having your antennae directed to, and beyond, the horizon allows leaders to pre-empt what is to come, to prepare for change and even to influence it.

Three Ego States in Transactional Analysis (TA)

So why include this aspect of TA in a leadership book? Well, at its simplest it gives us an insight into our and others' behaviours, and when considered with the work of Merrill and Reid, and Baddeley and James, can start to give us an understanding as to why some people behave as they do. More importantly, with that increased understanding may come alternative methods of influencing people more effectively.

The basic frame of the three ego states in TA can explain some fairly fundamental behaviour in human interactions and therefore can be of use in any situation where there is a need for understanding individuals, relationships, communication and systems.

TA has come from the work of Eric Berne (*Games People Play)* and Tom Harris (*I'm OK, You're OK*) and is based on the concept of three ego states.

Parent Ego State: Behaviours, thoughts, and feelings copied from parents or parent figures. The ego of learnt authority, which is frequently judgmental, often represented by 'you must do this', and possibly by pointing and finger wagging: parents know best.

Adult Ego State: Behaviours, thoughts and feelings that are direct responses to the here and now. This is the ego of rational thought and reason, which takes the facts and interprets and expresses them in a neutral and non-judgmental way.

Child Ego State: Behaviours, thoughts, and feelings replayed from childhood. The emotional child, this is the emotional state that is to do with internal reactions and feelings. One can think of it as being responsible for feelings of happiness or sadness that can't be understood and that usually come from your early years.

Interestingly TA describes that all of us have all three egos: child, parent and adult. However, they:

- May be in different proportions.
- May occur at different times.
- Occur in response to different transaction stimuli, which may trigger one ego or another, or even that the

same stimulus may trigger different egos depending on circumstances and perhaps your mood.

- Change swiftly from one to another.

It is an interesting exploration to recognise, when responding to others, what it is that trips us into parent mode, 'you will do' or allows us to remain in Adult mode. What is it that trips a childish response, is it because it touches an emotional state, and consequently bypasses rationality?

Even when we are working well, thinking logically and very aware of the here and now, in other words in full Adult ego state, what is it that allows us to be contaminated by the other states?

- Contamination of our Adult ego state by the Parent ego can happen unconsciously, for example, it could be when we talk as if something is a fact or a reality when really this is just our own belief or opinion. At best this can be light-hearted or amusing – have you ever said or quoted directly words your parents spoke, that you swore you would never use? Yet at worst, it can perpetuate racial or cultural stereotypes, 'all homeless people are drug addicts' or 'all police are crooked'.

- It could be that our Child ego state contaminates our Adult state with something, unconsciously or not, tapping into past feelings and emotions. Have you ever heard something said that sends a shiver down your spine, or immediately has you recalling an unpleasant past experience that interferes with you doing what you are doing in the here and now?

- We can get contamination from both Parent and Child ego states simultaneously, with one impacting upon and reinforcing the other. Perhaps when you get stopped for a minor speeding offence 'all police are crooked' (Parent) and you did once at the age of 8 get a reprimand from the local police officer that scared you (Child). This dual contamination of recalling the fear (that eight-year-old Child ego), and the unreasonable belief that 'all police are crooked' (Parent ego), will have an immediate effect on your behaviour in the Adult state.

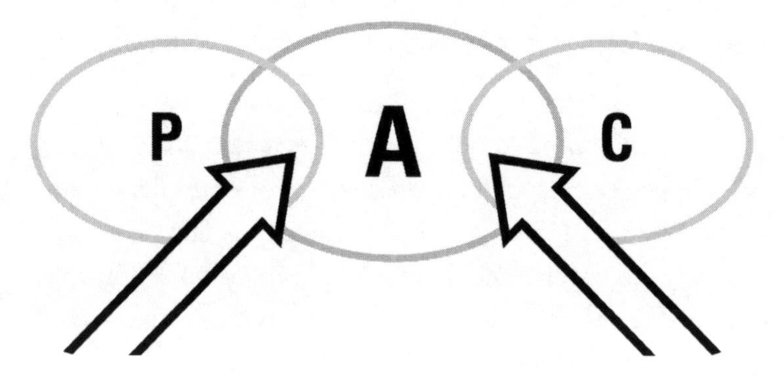

Contamination by Parent state   Contamination by Child state

In leadership, we would all like to think that we function in a constant Adult ego state; alas not. Importantly, those you may be leading will not be either, as other subtle and not-so-subtle experiences in their lives will lead them to respond to your behaviours in very different ways. Indeed, often it is only those people outside our situation, and sometimes outside our peer group or culture, who can see that objectively, and therefore can help us to see that 'our beliefs' are just that, 'ours', and therefore they can be changed.

'Hummmm, which ego state should I release on these people?'

In TA every interaction between individuals is a 'transaction'.

- The 'agent' is the one who speaks to the other and delivers a 'transaction stimulus'.
- The 'respondent' is the one who receives the spoken word or the action and sends back the 'transaction response'.

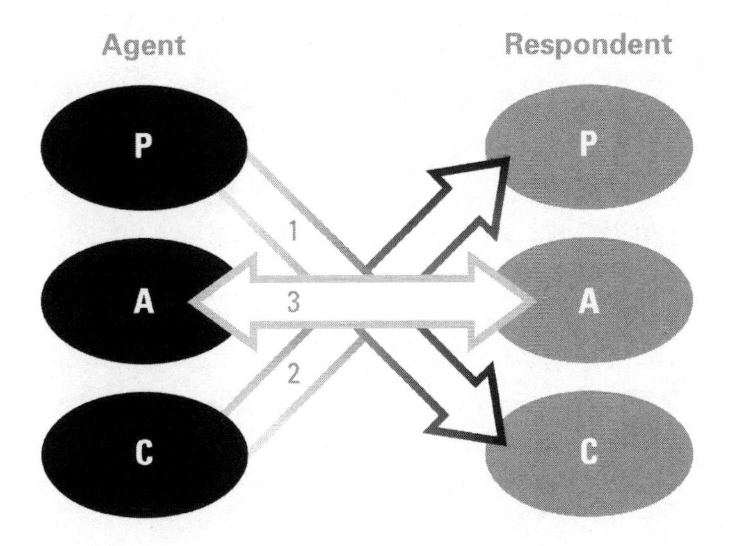

We would invite you to try to relate to the following states and consider when you may have experienced them, and indeed with this insight reflect back on what you may now do differently. TA examines each transaction as, 'I do something to you, you do something back'.

1. Parent Ego – talking to Child Ego

The leader taking the parent role could go two ways.

Supportive nurturing parent Wanting to protect or assist in the development of 'their team' (family) and at times this could be just what is needed for a team. Alternatively it could be received as smothering or overprotecting your team from the real world out there. 'It's OK, you don't need to worry about that, I'll take care of it and explain later'.

As a team member, how would you receive this? What might your responding behaviours be in return to being spoken to and treated in this way? Do you conform, 'Oh thanks I'm very grateful', nodding your head appreciatively, or do you rebel, 'No, I want to know what's going on, it affects me and I should have a say', with finger tapping impatiently on the table?

Controlling parent Knowing best what 'their team' (family) needs, and how to go about it. 'Right, Team, I've decided that because all our customers are ill informed and don't understand our product well enough, from Monday, everyone will start using this same profile to explain the benefits to each customer. And I don't want to hear of anyone not doing it this way.'

If you recognise this approach or have ever experienced it, take a moment to recall your response. In Child ego state it could be in two different ways: 'Yes, Boss' conforming and adapting to the immediate situation, or the free rebel asking, 'Why, who says that's the best way, I'm not doing that' and even if that wasn't said, it is what was going through your head and your behaviour showed it, head down, bottom lip protruding, foot tapping, sighing, no eye contact and that internal voice ultimately yelling 'Get me out of here, away from this numbskull'.

2. Child Ego – talking to Adult ego
The leader in child role

The free child Experiencing life playfully, responding in the immediate, laughing or crying as they go with their emotions, wanting to explore in a playful, inquisitive manner.

'OK, Team, ignore the policy for a moment, let's think outside the box and sod convention, if we get this wrong and miss our targets it doesn't matter.'

The nurturing parent response might be to give a warning: 'Be careful, you don't want to get yourself in trouble.' Yet the controlling parent response from the team around them could be a clear warning statement or even an ultimatum: 'All leaders who try to implement change in this way fail, we have seen this time and time again over the years, and we will not be part of it.'

The adapted child, responding to the immediate and adapting to it, often calls on previous experiences that affect behaviour. You've just been asked to give an update on progress towards targets for your entire division at the annual corporate event. Consciously or often unconsciously you have never been great at speaking to large audiences since you fell off the stage at high school. As you read the email, your pulse rate quickens, facial skin reddens, thoughts start to flutter all over the place, your drying mouth is in need of a drink and to top it all, your colleagues are just arriving for the meeting with you. What are they going to see sitting before them?

A nurturing positive parent response from them, before you have even spoken, could be 'Are you OK, can I get you a glass of water?', or to sit and think in judgmental parent mode, 'Who is this inadequate person, I knew they weren't up to the job'.

3. Adult ego to Adult ego

The theory is pretty simple, the solution and what to do about it less so, because so much is happening unconsciously. The beauty of the work of Transactional Analysis is that is gives us a tool to recognise it, and if we can recognise it, we may in turn be able to do something about it.

This will then enable the leader to stay consciously in the Adult ego state as much as possible.

The ability to stay in the here and now is very important, recognising how other things are affecting the situation, but not being governed by them: 'This has happened before, and we didn't handle it too well, we need to learn from that, yet look at this situation as a fresh challenge.'

It is important to use facts and known information to inform your thinking, and not rely on your or others' emotions. That stated, there is no excuse for ignoring emotion. The Adult ego state, at its very best, will recognise the benefit and impact of emotions on commercial and organisational decisions, and failure to do so could dramatically undermine progress in VIP: 'We need to consider how this will be received by the workforce. Such a significant decision will have an impact on many longstanding employees and we must consider how best to support them through transition'.

TA teaches that change is difficult when you are in either the Child or Parent mode, as these are similar, although in different ways, being neither rational nor fully thoughout.

Nevertheless, awareness of which ego we are in can allow us to change our behaviour in ways that are beneficial not only to ourselves but to those around us.

Hence TA can help by:

- Allowing us to identify which ego state we are in, so that we can move to another, if we choose.
- Allowing us to choose which ego state to use in the transaction response.

TA looks not only at words but also actions and behaviour, for example:

- The whining voice of a Child.
- The finger pointing of the Parent.
- The attentive pose of the Adult.

TA may allow you, not only to understand yourself, but also to understand those around you. We all have established patterns of behaviour with other people, some helpful and others less so.

Who is that person who may be more senior to you, or you perceive to be brighter than you, whom you automatically put in the Parent role, with you taking the Child persona? With whom do you automatically go into Parent role, allowing them, or even encouraging them to stay in Child role, and then say things like, 'I wish they would make their own mind up', 'they are so dependent on me' (and perhaps you on them?).

What we would ask of you is to consider the key relationships you have in your working life and think how they may be adjusted, how many are truly Adult to Adult, and how you can start changing the dynamic. How do others see you?

As a leader it can be important to understand how others view you. When things are not going smoothly in your leadership role, understanding those around you can become vital. The leader may benefit at times from maintaining some distance between him or herself and the rest of the team. However, this means that interpreting the reactions of others may become more difficult. It is not uncommon for others to regard you, the leader, as 'scary', which means that they may be afraid of you, your intellect, your authority, your popularity, your emotional impact or even your physicality.

It is not vital that you are liked as a leader, although it is necessary that you are respected and trusted, so that followers are able to follow not through fear, but through trust. Yet trust is often referred to as 'earned': what does this mean? Well, trust is a retrospective thing, do you meet a stranger and immediately trust them with your money, or your children, or with a confidence? No, something has to happen, for trust to 'develop', something often subtle yet demonstrable, that provides you with the confidence to place your faith in that other person. At its subtle best, it could be a smile or a reassuring nod when needed, or an action. Recalling the story of a woman who often sat in the same train carriage as a man on her regular journey into work. Finding him a little shifty-looking, she avoided eye contact with him. One morning, as she leapt off at her stop, he rose from his seat and pursued her down the platform. As she turned, heart pumping with some anxiety, he presented her with the purse she had dropped when leaving her seat. Was he shifty now? No, he'd become trustworthy, and indeed eye contact became a regular feature, even speaking to 'Mr Shifty'. A few weeks later, during conversation, she discovered he had left his wallet at home, and did not hesitate to lend him money, and was it presented back to her with thanks the following day? To be sure it was. It is also true in leadership that apparently small actions produce huge trust and commitment.

So another question to ask yourself is this: as a leader or potential leader, what actions demonstrate to those around you, that you are trustworthy?

We hope that you will use the concept of different types, to understand those around you, and thereby know how to derive the maximum benefit from their participation in VIP.

VISION

VISION

YOUR VISION IS CRUCIAL TO THE SUCCESS OF ANY planned outcome and indeed to your success as a leader. Whether that vision is entirely yours or the creation of those around you, visions need to be encouraged and owned. Here we will explore the intellectual honesty needed in vision, the sharing of visions and the creative strategies that will allow everyone to share in the critical thinking and creative freedoms required of great vision.

Ownership of the vision is essential, getting people's buy-in and commitment may take some work: the more influence they have on the vision, the greater the probability of ownership. So be careful not to assume that all visions are positive. Your idea of a positive vision, with a wonderful and glorious future ahead, could easily be another's nightmare of more change, difference and life upset. So the creation of a positive vision, that people want to move towards, is essential.

Everything starts with a thought or an idea. No matter how mundane or radical it might seem, it starts there. Successful leaders not only allow themselves to dream but learn to articulate that dream for others to share and subscribe to. It was Eleanor Roosevelt who said 'the future belongs to those people who believe in the beauty of their own dreams'.

Your VISION is likely to be most powerful if the outcome you intend to PRODUCE benefits not only yourself and your colleagues, but also those beyond. This may apply to producing a product for the greater good, while still meeting the desires you may have for commercial or financial success. There is another question that you may wish to ask yourself and that is:

What is VISION?

- What do you see things being like in the future?
- What needs to happen to get you there?
- Do you really care about it?
- Does it matter?
- Who else knows about it?
- Who else cares about it?
- Who else wants to do something about it?

These questions are very important and will start to determine whether your VISION is strong. Strong vision requires clarity of purpose and outcome, and enables you to:

✓ Be inspirational to others

✓ Lead with innovation

✓ Be resilient to setbacks and remain optimistic

✓ Empower those around you to have their own mini-VIP processes, within the overall aim, while sharing your dream.

So essential components of your VISION, that you should be able to articulate, would be:

- What is your VISION?
- What do you want to happen?
- Why is it so important?
- Who will benefit from what you PRODUCE in VIP?
  - You?
  - Your customer/client?
  - Your colleagues?
  - All of you?

To be more sophisticated in articulating the point, the question, 'What will the world be like when we have achieved our outcome through VIP?', is to convey, upfront how you, the customer, and your colleagues might experience the final vision, try using sensual language, in order that you are able to illustrate how . . .

- It would look different . . .

  What will others see and notice that would be an improvement?

- It would feel different . . .

  How could they expect to feel having achieved the vision: proud, satisfied, ecstatic?

- It would sound different . . .

  What feedback would they hear from others or what would they be saying to themselves on completion of the vision?

Time to be honest with yourself again: 'Am I the one to lead the VIP process?'

Are you asking yourself:

- Should I do it: are you considering this leadership role because you feel an obligation?
- Do I want to do it: are you genuinely enthusiastic and positive towards the ideas?
- Do I have to do it: is the vision yours, or is it part of a larger corporate direction/vision?

As you are developing your VISION, you will want to be sure as to where you are, and this leads to a further series of possible questions:

- Where do you really want to be?
- What is the difference between where you are now and where you want to be?

- Is this VISION part of something bigger, that you need to keep an eye on? In other words what is the bigger picture and how does is impact your own vision?
- How will you keep a check on your VISION?:

  - is it still there?

  - has it changed?

  - do you need to refine your Vision as part of the VIP process before moving into the next phase of *INVOLVE*?

Leadership in VISION

THE VIP STRUCTURE HELPS PROVIDE A SIMPLE FRAMEWORK to assist you in avoiding the pitfalls that might slow down the process of envisioning. So the challenge will be for you to use all your leadership skills both to define the VISION and to maintain your commitment and enthusiasm to it. There are some pitfalls to be avoided:

- It is possible to lose sight of the VISION by being stuck or weighed down by the present realities.

  Remember to stop, step back, and allow time for critical thinking.

  CRITICAL THINKING examines any assumptions, evaluates current evidence, re-assesses need (market), reviews key goals, and checks out beliefs and values.

- You may retain the *VISION* but not know how to move from the *VISION* to *INVOLVE* and *PRODUCE*

  Don't worry, create an additional vision as to how you will INVOLVE others and how they in turn will go on to PRODUCE

- You may come to doubt your role as the leader for the VIP process.
    - 'I'm not good enough to do this'
    - 'I don't really think it can make a difference'

  Rarely do we work with leaders who don't question this at some point, it's normal and can keep you grounded. Sit back, take stock, and get a good mentor or coach who will challenge you, keep you fresh, and reassure you of your capability.

These are potential 'ball and chains' that could slow you down. If significant problems remain with your VISION, then the wisdom of your VISION may have to be questioned or re-assessed.

So it's time to break free from the shackles, leave the ball and chain behind, and get your vision polished for the consumption of others.

'He was no visionary, and no matter how hard he tried, he just couldn't see a way out'

Shared ideas and visions

From VISION, the leader needs to move smoothly to INVOLVE. To some degree, the division into VISION, INVOLVE and PRODUCE is artificial and there will, inevitably, be some degree of overlap as one dissolves into the other.

To move from VISION to INVOLVE, your ideas within VISION need to INVOLVE others and become projects to PRODUCE. Therefore:

- 'Your VISION' needs to become 'Our VISION', so that those around you commit to INVOLVE
- Your idea of what is possible within 'Your VISION' may differ from the ideas of those around you. They may, at least at first, have a different VISION, which will lead to other outcomes that may be subtly or perhaps even totally different from yours. Any differences will need to be resolved, and this will require your leadership.
- By moving from 'Your VISION' to 'Our VISION' the process can move from 'Why should we make this happen?' to 'How do WE make it happen?'

Making Time for Creative Thought. Disney's VIP

LET'S PUT INTO PERSPECTIVE JUST WHAT WALT DISNEY achieved and when he achieved it. Now entertainment in the form of full-length feature animations are commonplace, yet in the 1930s, this genre was unheard-of. Creating experiences for whole communities where families could escape from reality and enjoy holidays in magical kingdoms in 1950s post-Second World War America must, by many, have been considered 'bizarre', 'not possible' or even 'mad'. Disney's theme parks are now commonplace, and often considered by many families across the world as some Mecca-like place that 'you must go whilst your children are young', and a 'rite of passage' experience, for youngsters and older people alike.

Robert Dilts studied work from previous conversations with Disney and distilled from his creativity this version of the 'Disney Strategy', which is a useful tool for practical creativity, either for individuals or groups, and indeed one often used by us (the authors) to free up organisational and political restraints, and to encourage leaders to unleash their creative powers.

Walt Disney was rumoured to use different rooms in his house for different aspects of his process. The principle being that different spaces, as well as skills, are needed to undertake different tasks. It turned out that Disney had a highly refined process for creating reality from dreams. Disney had three phases to his version of VIP, phases that were kept separate: a strategy still deployed to this day.

The Disney strategy

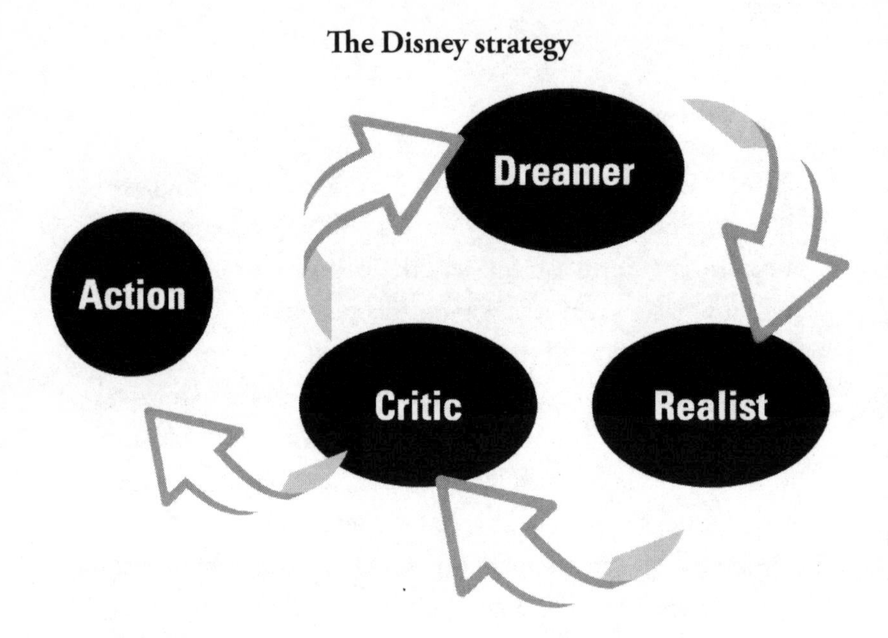

His three key phases were:

- **Dreamer.** Taking the concept of daydreaming: 'licensed to dream', not questioning the idea, just imagining what, at its very best, things could be like. Taking an idea, playing with it and expanding it without any constraints of reality.

- **Realist.** The next step was to look at the dream and decide what would be needed to turn it into reality.

- **Critic.** The critic then looks at the results of the realist and puts it under scrutiny. This might include Health and Safety issues, moral or ethical, or political or financial perspectives that would need resolving for success to happen.

- The idea was spun around all three areas three times. In order to keep it alive and creative, the project was given back to the Dreamer each time.

- Having spun through the Dreamer, the Realist, the Critic phases at least three times the challenge is to then move to Action.

So, it is perhaps easy to see how the Disney strategy is similar in concept to VIP. These processes can be used to create a new service, in research projects, and perhaps even in job searches. For example, you might dream what job you would like to have, then create a plan of how to turn that dream into reality, then allow the realist to develop your plan and what you will need to achieve to get there. The critic then critiquing your plan may discover flaws and explain that, in order to study philosophy at Oxford or Harvard, it is really necessary for you to complete specific aspects of study not currently taught within your secondary school. Well . . . back for the dreamer and realist to kick the idea around!

For organisations and leadership, the Disney Strategy is a great tool that fits smoothly with VIP. Create time for your team to dream in a space where imagination is not only tolerated but encouraged. From there move to another area to discuss practicalities of achieving that dream, without being distracted by obstacles that the natural critics in your team may identify. However, each member of the team is important and each dreamer, realist and critic, that works with you will get their time to shine in due time. As we highlighted looking at the work of Merill and Reid, the Analytical may be the Critic, and the Driver may be the Realist. Having taken it through critic, move it back to the dreamer, in order to keep your ideas alive, and creatively respond to the comments from the realists and critics. Three times around will leave you with some new, creative, and even excellent unexpected new ideas for implementation.

Once you are comfortable and confident of your VISION, it is time to seek out those you need to INVOLVE, and who will help you to fulfil your dream.

INVOLVE

Involve

THE BASICS OF INVOLVE ARE THAT:

- You will need those around you to be involved with and to share your VISION.
- You will need to establish good working relationships in order to INVOLVE
- You will need those around you to be committed to PRODUCE.

The principles of INVOLVE can be deduced from much of what we have already discussed:

- In order to INVOLVE, you as leader will need to consider when to ask people rather than tell them. The Amiables and Analytics identified by Merrill and Reid will not take lightly to being told, remember it is not their preferred way. If you always deliver in the mode of instructing and telling, those same individuals may well end up doing whatever you need to be done grudgingly or even not at all.

- If you have good relationships with those around you, INVOLVE will be easier than if your relationships are strained. Therefore try to foster the relationships with those whom you need to INVOLVE.
- Your light and your shadow are interesting concepts discussed by Radcliffe. You can view this concept from the two perspectives.
  - Your light is a nice analogy, with the idea being that your light shines on your colleagues: this is positive and builds a picture of the support that you offer.

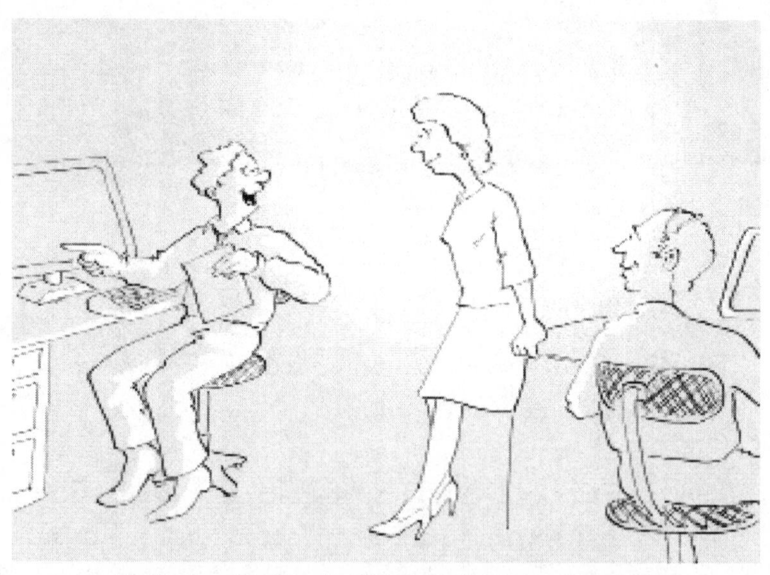

The leader who shines her light builds the team in INVOLVE

- Your shadow may be dark and menacing and feels, to those in the shade, as a significant negative influence.

The new boss oversaw the changes to the department

- Hence try to minimise your shadow and maximise your light.

Meetings will be a major activity for you as a leader, in order to INVOLVE those you need to help you PRODUCE. Meetings can be the bane of any project; taking up valuable time, providing a forum for conflict, achieving little and being perceived as holding back progress. How often have you listened to people complain about meetings at work, whether a one-to-one meeting, or a large team meeting involving consulting and discussion with others?
Meetings can also be the backbone of a good project or challenge; inspirational, a chance to air concerns or fears,

a time to explore the next steps and share progress or great practice. What would it be like to look forward to meetings knowing you had a tool to navigate more successfully through them? Well, in this section we hope to give you some tools and share some insights that will have you not only looking forward to your next meeting, but wishing you could put the book down and start it now.

We will cover how best to engage and get a rapport with others, through telling stories or building creative strategies. We will recognise the importance of power in organisations and explore a little how to influence, negotiate and assert what it is you need.

Storytelling – from VISION to PRODUCE

STORYTELLING, CREATING A COMPELLING DIALOGUE, CAN be a powerful tool that helps articulate the vision and gather momentum through into INVOLVE.

We listen to stories day in, day out, and they manifest themselves in so many different ways whether it is in the form of gossip or rumour, or just relaying your adventures at the end of the day to a partner. We listen to them, choosing to believe or dismiss them, as it suits our world at that moment.

There is something basic about stories, after all speech and dialogue existed way before the written word. It is as if somehow as a species we are hard-wired to tell and receive stories. When we were born, long before we could read, use laptops, or send texts, we learnt through listening to others relaying verbal information, tales, advice and instructions.

So, as we are all influenced by a good story, it is vital that, you as the leader are able to use storytelling as a tool in order to bring your vision to life, and thereby to allow others to understand and follow you.

Do you remember an inspirational teacher or instructor who influenced you? Didn't they use stories to bring their subject matter to life? Think of those friends and colleagues who can genuinely hold court and engage you, whether in the boardroom or round the dinner table, with tales that, in the hands of others, would just be mundane anecdotes.

'Gather around, Team, now just imagine a time when your bonuses are this big'

Somehow, as organisations become larger, corporate messages become more important and political correctness rules; stories in business become compromised and edited down to the 'core simple message'. Straightforward, easy-to-remember core messages that simply portray and define what you are about serve an important purpose, yet it is the story behind the product or task that gives it life and meaning, and asks you to be part of INVOLVE.

We are not advocating ignoring the importance of

correctness, or that you use stories that cause offence to others, yet stories need some freedom to allow them to be creative, so that they can tap into the imagination of those listening.

So why is it that corporate leadership often strips its messages of all meaningful, engaging language, whatever the business; global information technology, healthcare or engineering? There is a tendency to churn out monotonous, often meaningless 'management speak'.

This is why 'bulls**t bingo' as a concept exists. Some have the ability to anticipate the garbage about to be imparted during a business meeting, and can be so accurate that they can pre-empt the exact words and tick them off in a points-scoring game.

We have flown in too many 'helicopters' over 'burning platforms' to fall for all the jargon bouncing around the leadership world. It is true that well thought-through metaphors are fabulous for explaining things that are hard to articulate, however others are unhelpful, cheesy and the only further clarity you get from their use is confirmation that you want to poke the culprit in the eye with a sharp stick. We notice this trend that every other sentence we are 'moving forward' and so as we 'move forward' we wish to scream, no, let's move backward just for a change (the author's free child leaps out), which other way would we wish to move? The overuse of a phrase can make it redundant and meaningless.

As 'executive champions' and authors of this integrated leadership 'portfolio' we suggest 'moving forward' on 'our journey'. It would be unfortunate if, at this stage, we had to 're-engineer' the deliverables we listed at the onset of this 'mission critical' aspect of this 'life-changing' book on leadership. We are confident that by now, we are all 'singing from the same hymn sheet' and you 'have a heads-up' on where we are coming from, reducing the need to 'parachute in' any further 'world class' examples of . . . ouch . . . my eyes . . . '[Enough clichés for now. Editor]

The captain suspected they had been drinking management rum again

It is not unusual to find some opposition to the concept of storytelling in business, generally from those who choose to interpret it as somehow childish, or say that 'we can't just make stories up'. Get over it, there is nothing childish about this complex communication tool, and yes, stories can be made up, and therefore in some contexts may not be ethical to use, yet the best and most powerful stories are often those that reflect real life accurately.

It is important for the leader to choose stories carefully, they are powerful and not to be misused, although finding the right story in the right context for the right audience can take some thinking through. Good leaders create stories that reverberate around organisations and get remembered.

Winston Churchill is remembered for his wartime orations, and quoted and quoted, again and again, yet hardly remembered for his peacetime role as Prime Minister: the right words at the right time matter.

Stories give the opportunity to paint the picture for others, so they can better understand your vision, buy into it, become INVOLVED and commit to working in PRODUCE. They give the opportunity to tap into the senses of the listener (Touch Hear See Taste Smell) inviting them in to join and participate in the story, not just be the recipient of a lecture as to what the future could be like. Do you recall stories as a child, where you often weren't just a distant observer but were actually in there: you were the hero or heroine?

Constructing leadership stories

The ancient art of storytelling has certain predictable features.

- Structure: beginning – middle – end
- Good versus Evil, Baddies and Goodies
- A moral
- Thought-provoking messages
- Happy ending

So firstly, who is your audience and what do they need to hear from you? What is it you want to change and why?

Pull your audience, those you seek to INVOLVE, into a story that is 'gripping', that involves those people at an emotional level, and that paints the picture that is your VISION and is supported by brief well-chosen evidence.

Building a compelling story for change is a systematic process.

The story has to get attention and this can be achieved by making it personal, something that people can relate to, in that it refers to an individual. When the scale of things are so huge, such as the global aspiration of your company, it can be too detached from the reality of the life of the audience, whereas personalised stories break it down so that people understand and even directly relate to the issue. It is as if some things are too big or too distant to comprehend or relate to. An example would be when hearing on the news or in the media of human disasters, great famine, earthquakes, floods and tsunamis; the numbers suffering are just too vast to grasp, and impossible to comprehend. Yet often that one TV image that captures the suffering or death of that one individual child or family member allows us to relate to the tragedy, empathise with it and be glad it wasn't our family or child: we have become INVOLVED with the story. Now tell me the scale and I understand what it means. It is what happened in the Ethiopian famine of the 1980s when Bob Geldof, touched by those single human story images, had a VISION, INVOLVED celebrities and others in PRODUCE, and the result was Live Aid, which gave the public a sense of purpose in putting something right.

In order to attract the attention of those listening to the story, often the story may need to start by delivering something shocking, perhaps sometimes graphically tragic, to get their attention and wake them up – 'wow, I wasn't expecting that', or 'we usually get some boring corporate objective session'. Having painted the picture of what it is like, invite the listener in; 'Could you imagine what that is like?', 'How would you feel if . . . ?'

Now turn the story around, tell them what it could be like, what it really could look and sound like, and how it could feel very different. Invite the listeners into the new story in order to help them realise the VISION that you have, and now hopefully they are starting to share it or at the very least have a greater understanding of it. By creating this new picture and then inviting people into this alternative world, to 'imagine how this feels', the dream, your VISION can become a perceived reality (their VISION), and they become part of INVOLVE, and thus VIP starts to be achievable.

There are many formulas you can use to create a good executive story, but what is certain is that it has to come from you, be genuine and authentic. The listener or follower will sniff out an over-rehearsed formulaic story. We suggest our eight-point guide with the components:

1. Get the listeners' attention	Say something shocking, positive or negative *'This could be a failed product'*
2. Give something of yourself	Disclose your own belief, options, thoughts, feelings or own story. *'I remember such a poor experience many years ago and it affected my perception of this kind of product for years.'*
3. Invite them into the story	Tap into their emotions *'Imagine how you would feel to experience this kind of service'*
4. Tell them what it could be like	Start to paint an alternative picture. *'It needn't be like this, with real effort what we could do is . . .'*
5. Paint a compelling new picture	Build on your VISION and invite them into a new world. *'Just imagine . . .'*
6. Give logic and reason	Use evidence statistics or useful information. *'Over 60% of our customers have expressed the view that . . .'*
7. Give a corporate message	Link your story to the purpose of the organisation *'This is in-line with our company values that state . . .'*
8. Happy ending	Remind me again of what it will be like when we achieve this *'So rather than a failed product our customer will be confident that their . . .'*

Power, Organisations and Leadership

UNDERSTANDING PEOPLE AND HOW THEY GAIN AND HOLD power can often be puzzling, sometimes inspiring, and not unusually perceived as wrong or unfair.

There are many ways that power can be used or abused in any organisation:

1. Delegated power – that comes with the responsibility of the role/position a person occupies.
2. Expert power – knowledge, experience or qualification based.
3. Information power – I know something you do not, or have access to an information source that you don't.
4. Productive power – my sales are higher than yours – I'm more productive than you.
5. Connections power – I'm well networked and know them well.

6. Purse power – I hold the money or access to it.
7. Relationship power – I'm in or have had an 'intimate' relationship with another influential person.
8. Political power – I'm in an elected position, the people want me.
9. Related power – the boss is my father.
10. Long service power – I've worked here for years.
11. Popularity power – I'm loved among the workforce.
12. Dauphin power – heir to the throne, I'm next.

People may have one or more of the power status positions and deserve them through hard work, dedication and commitment; others may have inherited some of these power positions.

There are always those who misuse the power, usually for their own selfish purpose rather than for the good of others or the organisation.

The problem of perceived power

There is, in addition, the strange existence of Assumed Power, where the individual believes they are powerful and hold power, whilst those around them perceive quite the opposite. Although this can be, at times, amusing or even hilarious to observe and often invites ridicule, be careful as assumed power can at times be a damaging force.

The effective leader understands power, acknowledges power and works with it or, at times, challenges power, as they increase their own ability to influence and develop positive power. This may sound a little Machiavellian, yet to be blind to where power sits is a naive and potential career-limiting place to be.

Knowing where power sits is important, as positive and negative power games are played, even in the healthiest of professional environments. However, be careful, as to engage in power games is often the downfall of many with potential. Understanding the power game and peoples' motives is one thing, joining the game is quite another.

Good leadership observes, notices, and even takes into account the impact and consequences of power from various sources. Yet to enter the power game fullly can be extremely disempowering, as it is possible that you fully become part of the problem rather than the solution.

Think of it like a game of chess. To play chess effectively you must have a clear overview of the board, almost be detached from the game, looking at the pattern of the pieces, thinking through your strategy and anticipating or responding to your opponent. So remaining high above the board with that overview is essential.

So, the leader who becomes embroiled in the power games ultimately disempowers themselves; it is like being

drawn down into the game rather than seeing it for what it is. Imagine trying to play chess from eye level to the board. It is almost as if you are on the board and can't see the queen or the knights (or wood for the trees) and that you become a piece and part of the game, and are part of the various moves, rather than orchestrating them.

So within VIP's INVOLVE, understanding power, where it lies, and its relative impact on your chance of moving to PRODUCE, is important.

Power mapping
– plotting your way through the power maze

Understanding Spheres of Influence

Any leader needs to be able to plot out how people and groups of people around them influence each other, discovering where real power in a complex environment lies. Power can often be in unusual or unexpected places and not connected at all to designated hierarchies or formal lines of management. It is probably true to say that hierarchies usually define accountability rather than power. There are certain important stages in power mapping.

1. It is worth simply plotting out who has direct influence on what it is you wish to achieve, asking do they have a direct influence on this being achieved, or when achieved would this have a direct influence on them? Or of course both.

2. Map outwards, by placing the outcome in the centre and mapping the most influential people close to the centre, then ask yourself who influences them, adding these people to your map. If you wish you can keep going mapping out just who influences whom. See diagram opposite

3. By mapping this out you can start to look for paths of influence. This allows you to be efficient as you look to gain support, and INVOLVE people in your VISION. Doing this simple exercise, early in any process, can give fascinating intelligence and prevent hours of frustration contacting or trying to engage the wrong people.

   Now look at the map and mark on it:

   - Critical influencers: the final decision makers, deal breakers/makers.
   - Key influencers: those with a strong voice, who are listened to, credible, and without whom it is

unlikely that your VISION will go-ahead or be a success. Their support or involvement is vital as they sit around the critical influencers and this often makes them the most influential of all.

- Marginal influencers have influence in relatively small parts of the proposed action, yet taken together they can have a big impact on decisions.
- No influence; actions will go ahead or not regardless of their view (be honest about who these people really are, there can be more than you think).

4. Now take a good look at the map. Who are the people who share your VISION, with whom you need to fully engage in order to INVOLVE in your pursuit of the final goal you will PRODUCE?

Don't be fooled into following the traditional hierarchy of influence, for example, concentrating on those who are most senior, as it may be worth getting a critical mass of support first. If your working relationship isn't sound or established with any key influencer, look around to see who influences them: could you work with them to gain greater influence?

Your idea may be the best in the world and make complete logical sense; even so, human networks and systems don't usually work on logic; who presents the idea is far too often more important than the idea itself.

When you have mapped out the important people it is

Place around the outcome those who have a direct impact on it being achieved and those who it will have direct impact upon.

Then map out those who influence the people who have direct impact

Then those who influence them

Then add arrows to represent the direction of influence

They have a direct impact on it being achieved (inward arrows)

When achieved it will have a direct impact on them (outward arrows)

They both have an impact on it being achieved and it will directly impact them on achievement

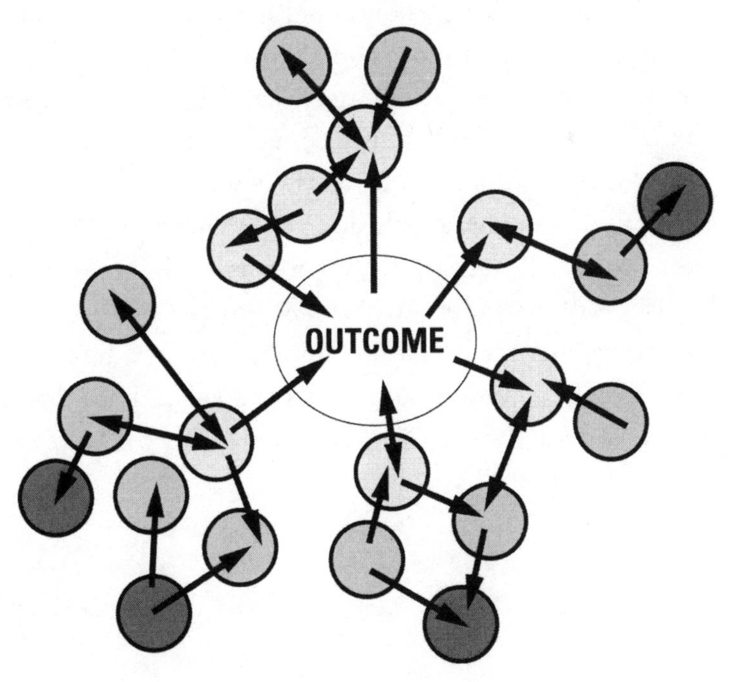

worth noticing, from your perspective, what kind of power they hold, and whether you can overlay that with what kind of political animal you believe them to be, Fox, Owl, Lamb or Donkey.

This exercise can provide a greater insight if you do it with another trusted colleague or small team who can challenge or agree with what are simply your perceptions.

The information gleaned may not only give you a pathway for getting your VISION adopted by others, it may even give you new ideas of how to influence those people who may not be immediate converts or advocates of your plans.

For example, think how you could best communicate with or involve with a Key Influencer, who likes to use Productivity and Popularity Power to influence others, yet is also a Fox.

Well, from the beginning, the Fox will need to know what is in it for him or her; how could it make them be more productive and gain more popularity? Get them on board by presenting this to them, rather than relying on moral or ethical reasoning, and then they may just do the work of persuading the critical influencers for you.

If all this sounds a little devious or underhand, well, it could be. The Leader aspiring to be a respected Owl should do this with absolute integrity and for the right reasons, another good reason to INVOLVE others, and be totally open in your approach and the greater good of the outcome, not simply your personal gain (you sneaky Fox you).

Strategy in INVOLVE

Within VIP your role as the leader is to set the VISION, then oversee the process of INVOLVE. The temptation to become the manager and become overly involved in the detail may be ever present. So how will you put in a structure that enables you to ensure that you remain in the overseeing role? It is your VISION and you have the right people INVOLVED, now allow them to PRODUCE.

The strategic task for the leader is to set the direction and scope of the organisation over the long term. This in turn requires insights and knowledge of the organisation through its configuration of resources, and ensuring a clear focus on priorities.

Strategy documents vary in style from complex multi-layered documents that become almost biblical tomes giving companies defined directions, to short aspirational documents that state, in brief, the organisation's intentions and future direction. Whichever is the case, process versus creativity are often in conflict.

Bob Bird, a leadership development expert, describes it as this:

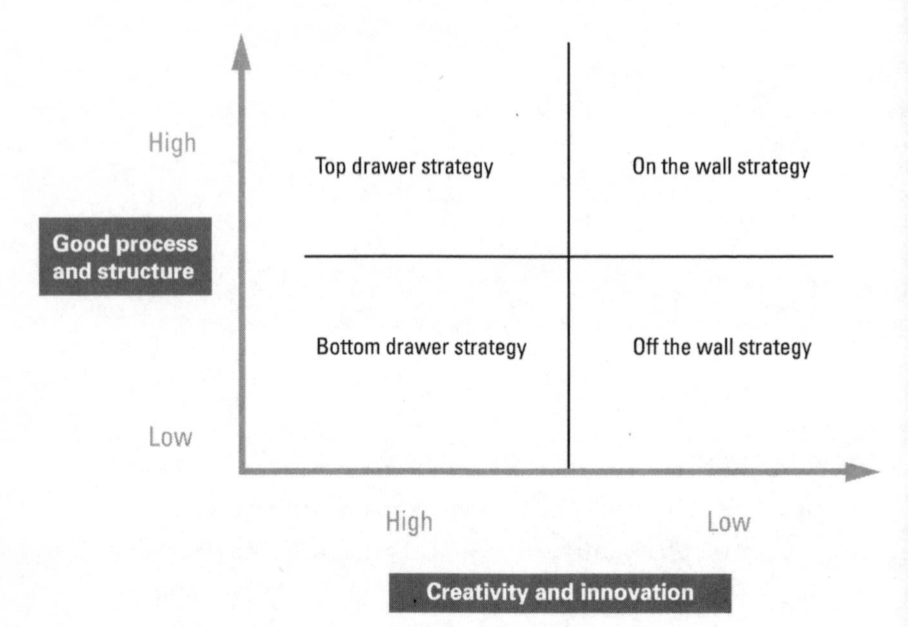

Bottom drawer strategy – Low in process and low in creativity, often gets produced as a matter of course, 'time to submit our annual strategy', and consequently it gets placed very quickly in the bottom drawer never to see the light of day again. It could be viewed as unproductive 'box ticking'. We recognise this and also recall each year agonising over the layout and construct, constantly believing that this would be the blueprint for activities over the next 12 months, staying up late into the early hours and ensuring it lands on the right person's desk within the time allotted, then never seeing the damn thing again.

Top drawer strategy – Good process and structure with clear methodology often taking huge amounts of effort to produce. It is taken out of the top drawer periodically to use as a measurement tool, by a primary motivator, to assess progress towards targets: the, 'it's July, are we where we predicted we would be?' discussions. Yet there is absence of, VISION, aspiration or anything new, and it is therefore seldom inspirational, unless of course you are inspired by the thought of being dismissed for not hitting your target, hum, we think not.

Off the wall strategies – Creative and potentially inspirational, yet so far from reality, and with no clear outline as to how it could be achieved, gets laughed out of the office and even ridiculed for being literally too 'off the wall'. It lacks the process and structure needed and therefore the bright ideas and aspirations become drowned by the 'are you having a laugh' and 'we can't do that' comments.

On the wall strategies – great vision, introducing new innovative and desirable outcomes, which are deliverable. There is clear VISION, identified people to INVOLVE and clearly defined and realistic approaches and timescales to PRODUCE. The final outcome is displayed on the wall in prominent positions, defining the future and displaying the clear milestones to be achieved for the organisation in order to reach its full potential within the agreed timescale.

The Environment and the Culture

WHILE THE VISION CAN BE STRONG EVEN IF THE GROUND is not fertile, the VISION may not germinate during INVOLVE and grow to PRODUCE. Therefore, assessing the environment is most important.

The concept of organisational culture is nothing new and well studied in the subject of Organisational Development (OD). Indeed most people will be familiar with the notion that there are different kinds of culture depending upon various factors including the product, the industry, its workforce demographics and its global location.

Some cultures are common in various organisations and well expressed in terms like 'blame culture', 'macho culture', 'culture of high-achievement', 'development culture', 'green culture' and so on.

Cultures are created within organisations and should be known and understood by the leader. Do you like the culture of your organisation? Do you wish to change it?

There is a great industry based on external consultants coming in and telling you just what is wrong with your

'Hey squirt, I will not tolerate a bullying culture in this company!'

culture, yet the mature approach is surely to explore it and understand it yourself, perhaps with some external support. The culture is of your making and don't underestimate the leadership's responsibility to influence it. Are the behaviours of the leaders consistent with the culture you want to have, or do you just talk a good game because you are bright and you have read a few leadership books?

Consider the leader who, having discovered through the workforce questionnaire that many people believe there is a bullying culture, declares to their senior team, 'This must stop, it's intolerable, and if you don't sort it within the next three months heads will roll, it's a product of your poor management styles, now get out of my office and don't report back to me until it's sorted'. Sounds like they have led by example and done a wonderful job of creating just the culture that others are now responsible for trying to change. Good luck.

What kind of culture do you need? It may be useful for you ask yourself these questions?

- Is there a 'Yes' culture?
- Is there an 'Ideas' environment?
- Are relationships healthy?
- Is communication really 'two-way'?
- Can people be heard from wherever they are?

As leader, it will be necessary for you to evaluate any limitations to your environment and assess whether they can be corrected, enhanced or developed before you seek to INVOLVE those around you. In other words, is your Vision achievable within the existing culture and are they ready to be INVOLVED?

What kind of rituals and routines do you have in place that reveal the culture you want (or indeed don't want)? What routinely happens within your systems and processes that demonstrates that culture? The very simplest levels of courtesy, for example, making yourself readily available to your colleagues, and saying 'please' and 'thank you', will show your respect and gratitude for their efforts.

The Involvement Spectrum

HAVING CREATED YOUR VISION, YOU MIGHT SIT BACK and wait for the clamour of approval. However, within the group you seek to INVOLVE, there will be a variety of responses, depending on the personalities and the experiences of those you talk to.

Radcliffe describes the involvement spectrum.

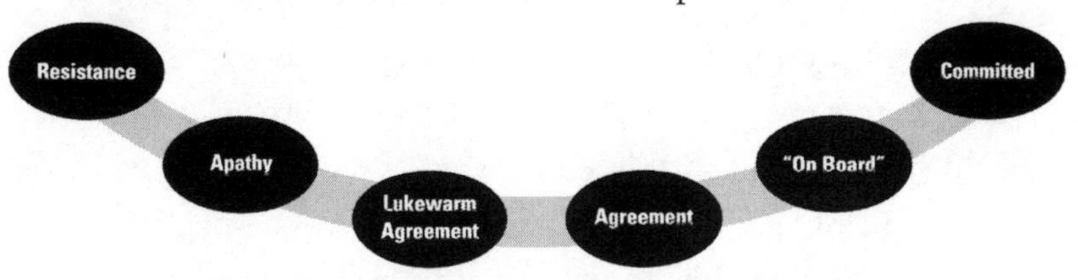

Radcliffe's involvement spectrum

In some ways this is like the Change Curve that we will discuss under PRODUCE.

- **Resistance** – At this stage, some around you may actively work against you.

- **Apathy** – By definition, at this stage, these individuals don't care.
- **Lukewarm agreement** – This can be analogous to the assembly line worker who accepts his or her job but doesn't enjoy it.
- **Agreement** – At this stage, those around you are the good soldiers who follow you unquestioningly.
- **'On board'** – Now your team is becoming enthusiastic but can still be distracted by issues within the team or from outside the VIP project.
- **Committed** – Now you can rely on the team. They will support you even when there are problems.

This spectrum of response in the INVOLVE phase of VIP is only to be expected. By using the methods we have identified to understand better differing personality traits or preferred types, it will often be much easier for you to understand why they are thinking, feeling and behaving in the way they do, and to modify your strategies to INVOLVE those whose help you need to PRODUCE.

None of us like to deal with negatives, especially if someone is negative about something you own or think is a worthy thing to do. Having stated this, it is obvious that, on occasions, it is essential; at least in the interests of intellectual honesty, if for no other reason, to highlight or define the negative put to you as warranted, or if not, at least acknowledge how you feel about the ideas.

The leader, when dealing with or delivering negatives to others, has a challenge, how can they do that honestly, with integrity and yet avoid de-motivating the recipient? There is an old adage that you must say four nice things about a person before you say anything negative or critical. There is much more than a grain of truth in this and of course, in our everyday dealings with our children, partners, parents and work colleagues, in order to be effective, we praise first and criticise second. As a leader you will find your own methods of dealing with this. However, the message is straightforward: THINK IT THROUGH FIRST.

With such a strong belief in people and people's potential to change and adapt, given the right set of circumstances and the right leader, we are reluctant to make the following comment. Our hesitation comes not because we do not stand by what we say, more that we are afraid of the leader who may be currently challenged by individuals and feeling stuck, and may have a lack of personal insight into their own behaviour and perceptions. That person may just put a greater emphasis on this next statement than most.

However, it is true that sometimes, no matter how great our understanding, or our attempts to make things right for people, some people find change just too hard and perhaps even impossible. So yes, in the right context, we do ultimately support the old saying, 'if you can't change the person, change the person': in any organisation there is a limit as to how far it can go in adapting to others in order to ensure their commitment. Yet, if you think all can be sorted by sacking individuals, and this is all you take from this book, then you are no leader.

Asking in INVOLVE

When looking at INVOLVE, asking is one of the big messages. From Merrill and Reid's types, it is true that the Analytics and the Amiables need to be asked. This will allow them to:

- More readily share your VISION so it becomes OUR VISION
- Move together with you to PRODUCE

By asking, you are also starting to set priorities, so you are:

- Asking for agreement (deals)
- Agreeing the focus and the priorities

By focusing on asking and agreeing, inefficient work should be prevented that might otherwise lead your team up blind alleys during PRODUCE.

Building relationships in INVOLVE

You will not be able to move through PRODUCE without the committed co-operation of those around you. It is here that your relationships with the team are at their most important. Your relationships will improve if you:

- Ask and don't tell. We make no apologies for repeating and reiterating this fundamental point. There is always the need for clear direction and at times even clear instruction, yet the clear request is stronger than the 'you must do'.
- Ask for what you really need and don't be afraid to be honest. You may care to reflect on our comments about intellectual honesty.
- When you ask clearly, then it is reasonable to expect a commitment in return: a deal – what can they ask of you, for example?
- By seeking advice from those around you, the solutions become "Our Solutions" and INVOLVE becomes increasingly meaningful.
- When you listen, those around you can start to feel part of your VISION and become committed to seeing it through.

Asking, seeking advice and listening make you, as the leader, a safe and trustworthy person who deserves a committed team

Rapport in INVOLVE

ALBERT MEHRABIAN, IN A WELL-CONDUCTED STUDY, CAME to a conclusion that will surprise many of us – that when communicating the message it is received as follows:

- The words of the message (content): 7%
- The intonation by which the message is delivered: 38% (voice pitch and tone)
- The facial expression of the person delivering the message: 55%

Although the work has been often challenged, there is much to it, and it has huge implications for the way that you, as a leader, deliver your messages in VIP, whether in story form, casual conversation or formal presentation. It also reinforces that, as a leader, you are seldom 'off duty' and that dropping your guard by a slight sigh or hunching of the shoulders can send an unintended message that can do more harm than good.

It is also useful to add insights from Peter Hawkins, Chairman of Bath Consultancy Group, where for the past 25 years he has been helping organisations in many parts of the world to connect their strategic change with their organisational culture and their leadership development. He has written extensively about leadership, leadership teams, coaching and supervision, including, *The Wise Fool's Guide to Leadership* and *Short Spiritual Stories for Organisational and Personal Transformation.*

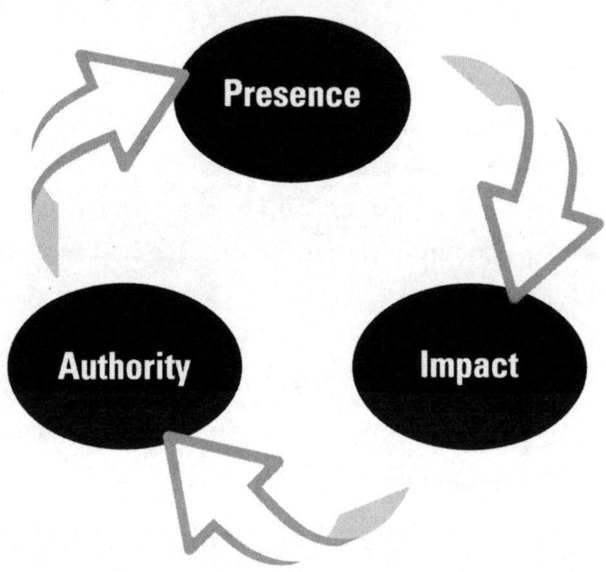

We access his insights around the authority of the leader, their presence, where they own the space and role of the leader, and then the impact that their intervention has. We can then start to explore these three states in relation to the effective leader and VIP. We feel it adds a valuable insight into the leader and proves a great development tool. Each element has an impact on the other, and by polishing and addressing each in turn, the concept starts to ensure that a competent leader emerges.

We have taken this framework and with our additional comments would ask you to think of your own leadership qualities in the context of each of these three areas. How would you rank them? Which is your stronger and which needs more work? When coaching even the most senior, experienced and competent leaders this framework is a great prompt for challenging discussions.

We will define the three further:

Authority – Being comfortable with the responsibility of the leader.

1. Awarded authority – that comes with a position or responsibility of the role you hold, often awarded to you by others.
2. Internal authority – that which you give yourself, the mindset where you give yourself permission to lead.
3. Authority of the subject matter – knowing what you are talking about.

Presence – being comfortable in your own space as leader

1. Present with yourself, by which we mean, knowing what you want and what you are feeling about the issue under discussion, and recognising the consequences of that. Having good personal insight.
2. Present with others, which means being in rapport, being there in the room when you are talking to and engaging with those you wish to INVOLVE and making sure you are open to their influence. This

means paying attention to their body language, to their pitch and tones of voice and, of course, the content of what they are saying, and being attuned to their emotional reactions as much as to their considered verbal responses. This is about the way you appear, and is related to your body language, such as whether or not you seek and maintain eye contact. In addition to eye contact, there are certain physical features of rapport:

- Head nodding
- Smiling
- Mirroring the body language of the individual you are talking to
- Mirroring the tone of voice of that person
- Using their name
- Reflecting back to them what they have said to you

3. Presence in the system is being well networked into and across the system. Do people know where you are, what you are achieving, what your ambitions are, etc?

Impact – Being able to utilise and positively exploit your role as the leader

As the leader you have impact, you bring something to the table, and you are not just a participant or bystander to conversations or decisions, but an influencer whose contributions have meaning and consequences. This establishes that the leader is much more than just a contributor to a dialogue, you have that 'something' that develops an idea, moves it forward, makes decisions and progresses it: you have the impact to achieve VIP.

That impact is not purely about the content of your interventions, it includes the energy you bring with it, including moving the required energy to areas that require development. 'Great idea, and what we could do further is . . . and I for one as managing director will support you all the way'.

Staying impactful

Problems can arise when your Vision becomes 'exclusively yours' or even 'possessively yours', when an almost childlike inner self kicks in with the 'that was my idea' syndrome. So, getting to the point of it being a shared VISION, as we have said, is vital. It does not necessarily mean that every aspect of your VISION is right or in any way perfect. Hence allowing others to correct and refine your VISION is an important aspect that can be easier said than done.

So you have your Vision, your desired outcome, and you need others on board to help you get there (INVOLVE).

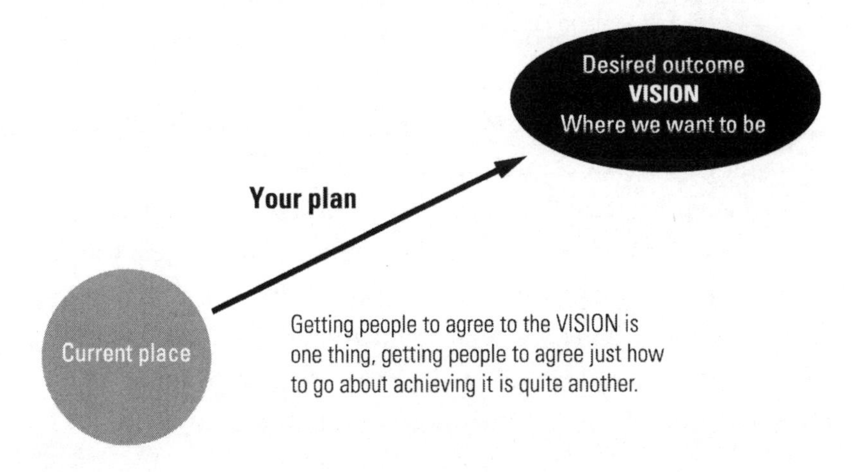

Influencing people has two key aspects –

1. Getting them to agree and buy into the VISION.
2. Getting people to buy into getting INVOLVED in the process allows you to build the strategy for PRODUCE.

It is interesting to notice that while coaching, most people put a greater emphasis on one or another of these. The effect being that those who spend a great deal of time creating and promoting the vision may succeed in getting initial buy-in, yet how do you achieve the VISION unless you have spent time on INVOLVE with those expected to PRODUCE?

Whilst working with a small organisation it was great to see them create a VISION that involved pulling a group of small companies together to work to PRODUCE an improved product. Even the optimistic coach thought it a tough job, yet they did it, pulling together and creating a combined VISION so that their combined strength could influence the market and in turn create a very successful enterprise. Yet only a few months into the venture the coach is contacted and invited back in to assist in 'retrieving the situation'. The business case was proven, the VISION worth signing up to, so why the problem? On arriving and talking to all parties, it became apparent that the INVOLVE stage had been neglected and ways by which they had to get to their desired outcome had not been negotiated and each had their own very different view on how PRODUCE would be achieved. With help, they pulled it around and managed to find a way all could agree on: the delay it caused, by not using a VIP process, had put the whole venture at risk.

In contrast, working with another organisation it was interesting to notice their well-defined agreed plans of action, with all parties apparently signed up to be INVOLVED. However, at a later date, it became clear that each had very differing views as to where they thought the actions were taking them. The lack of clarity and vagueness of the shared VISION allowed them each to create their own idea of PRODUCE, and these very diverse ideas ultimately led to the failure of the project.

These two examples may seem extreme, yet they are surprisingly common. Ask yourself where you put most of your attention; is it in the VISION, or in INVOLVE which is vital in order to develop the strategy to PRODUCE? Balance and harmony between the VISION and INVOLVE is important.

Negotiating in INVOLVE

For the first time we mention the word 'negotiate' and to do so, by definition, implies that there must be choices, options, and alternatives. So, if you think you know best how it should be achieved, and you think your way is the only way, then you may have problems!

The word negotiation is a much-misused word. It sets up an immediate expectation, if someone says they are coming to you to negotiate a particular issue/outcome with you, that somehow you have an influence and that there will be an agreement or way forward found that is somewhere between what they and you wish. The leader should never forget this expectation.

Within companies or large organisations, VISION may not be negotiable. Referring back to trust, if you set an expectation, deliver on it, if you say you are going to negotiate then do so. If for whatever reason the VISION or outcome is not negotiable then don't say it is, as this is a sure way to increase frustration, suspicion and lose much-needed trust. As Henry Ford famously and successfully declared when launching the very first mass-produced car. 'You can have any colour, as long as it's black.'

It is important that leaders put an emphasis and energy into getting others to agree and buy into the VISION. Then to get people to buy into and become INVOLVED in the method by which you will achieve the ultimate outcome – the strategy to PRODUCE.

When the VISION has clarity, and is confirmed, the aspect that is always up for negotiation is HOW to get there. The danger is that if you hold 'my way is best' you are becoming overly precious and have probably stopped listening to those around you, and you could then go on to micromanage and become overly controlling. There is no doubt that there is a balance to be achieved, as over-consultation and prolonged discussions could delay or interrupt production and be agonising for all involved. Yet this should not be used as an excuse for the leader to become too dogged and determined that their way is best.

Chunking: Starting from a Point of Agreement

Chunking is not an easy word; it simply refers to the levels of detail a leader focuses on. A 'big chunk' is high level broad principles, and a 'small chunk' is detailed descriptions and actions.

Chunking is an essential tool in INVOLVE and is about finding a point of agreement at the start of negotiations, thus allowing discussions to start from a positive agreement.

We can use the concept of chunking in two ways. We can:

- Become more **general** and get a bigger picture, by chunking up.
- Become more **specific** and get more detail, by chunking down.

So the art of Chunking is either to move from more general or abstract pieces of information down to more specific or detailed information, or, when required, to do just the opposite and take people who are stuck in detail up to a more general or abstract concept.

In studying the different personalities and types, it is clear that some people are more comfortable with the abstract, and others with more analytical preferences are more at ease with detail and scrutiny. There is a danger that when the leader has thought through their VISION, and understands in some detail their strategy, that they will launch into detail too soon and the more detail there is, the more there is for others to find fault with, disagree with, or just simply to comprehend.

Regardless of how different or divided people are, the skill of chunking up and asking the bigger questions has the effect of lifting discussions to a point of agreement. No matter how general or abstract that point of agreement might be, starting from approval is a much more healthy and productive place than starting from a point of disagreement or conflict.

Taking discussions upward to the broader principle gives discussions a sound place to start even though at times the agreement may be so abstract and principled that it is almost impossible to disagree with, such as:

'We need to produce a product that doesn't cause harm to others.'

'Our company needs to communicate effectively with its client base.'

If we widen this concept to cover everyone, it becomes clear fairly quickly that some people (and therefore some leaders) like to talk in generalities pretty much most of the time and others like to talk about everything in very detailed terms.

Although most of us can do both, our choice of level of detail, aside from preference, could be dependent on other

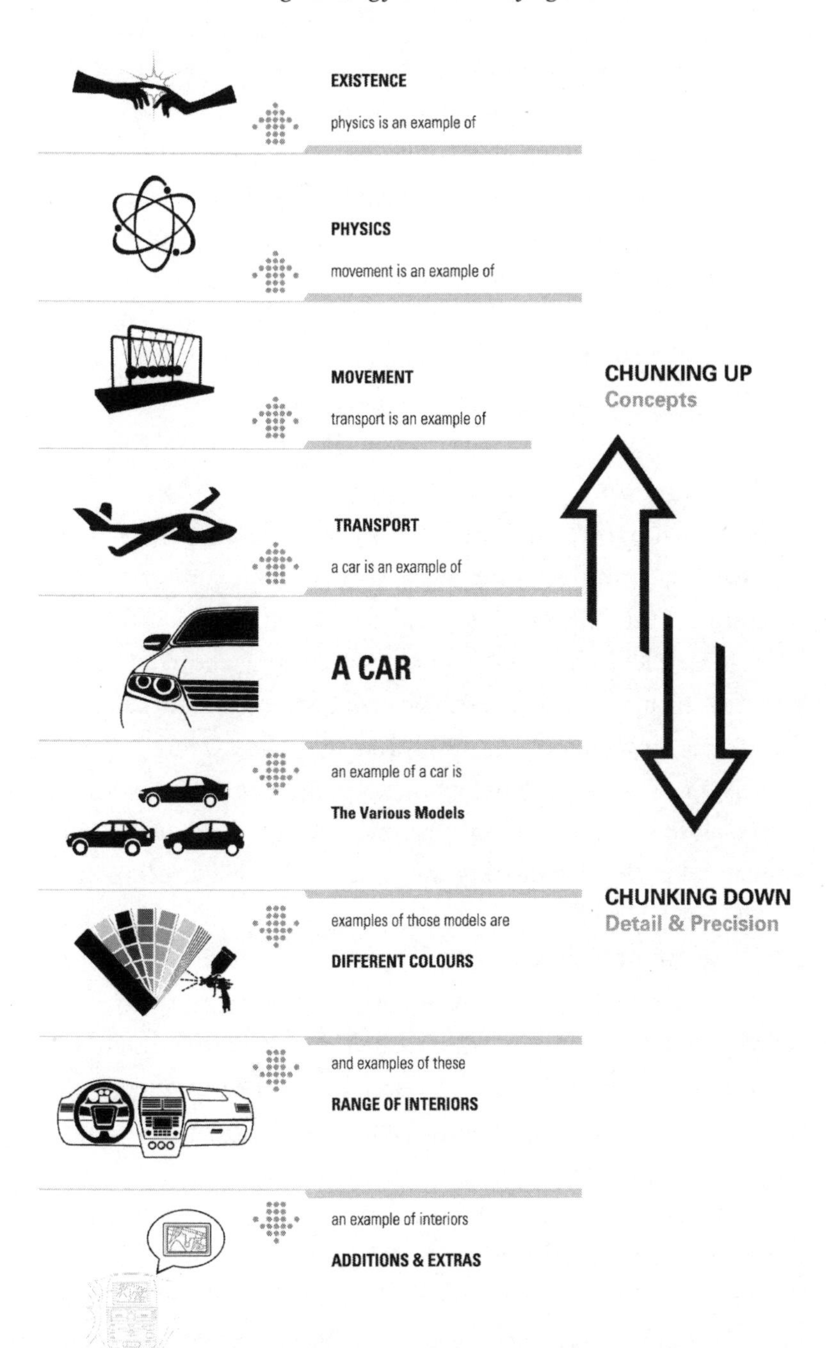
EXISTENCE
physics is an example of
PHYSICS
movement is an example of
MOVEMENT
transport is an example of
TRANSPORT
a car is an example of
A CAR
an example of a car is
The Various Models
examples of those models are
DIFFERENT COLOURS
and examples of these
RANGE OF INTERIORS
an example of interiors
ADDITIONS & EXTRAS
CHUNKING UP
Concepts
CHUNKING DOWN
Detail & Precision

factors such as the subject matter and your interest in it or your level of responsibility and accountability.

Developing the ability to recognise the chunk you are at, and moving people from it, is a required skill of a competent leader. Reaching agreement in a big chunk allows processes to start from a point of agreement and to gain acceptance of the broad outcome you want to achieve, before entering the process of defining the strategy of how the task will be carried out, when you have to go into more detail.

Chunking up.

It is an important and essential skill for the leader to know when to chunk up, and to be able to choose the level of 'chunk' that is needed to achieve agreement in order to inspire others with the bigger picture. Having chunked up to a high principle or a more abstract concept, the harder skill is to then slowly 'lose altitude and reduce height', moving the concept into more detail while keeping people on board. If you 'lose altitude too fast' and drop straight into detail you may take the idea quickly into a conflict zone and fall out around detail.

'So we need to communicate more effectively with our client base [all nods in agreement], so that means that every Wednesday at 3pm you go through your client contact list and personally phone each person' [no nods, just questions: why Wednesday? my client prefers emails, Friday mornings are better . . . why . . . why . . . why?]

Therefore, one of the most useful ways to avoid disagreement is to reduce the level of detail and talk about principles and generalities from the start.

'We are here today to ensure the future financial stability

of the organisation' – a big chunk and a clear starting place.

Moving down – 'We have to bring down our current expenditure on non-essential equipment and reduce waste.'

Moving down – 'We have to find a way of doing that without reducing the quality of our product.'

Overcoming an argument by chunking up toward generalities and away from detail is a tactic that can be used at various points of interventions. When talking strategies with staff or other organisations, agreeing the big chunk is an important place to start.

Another example could be:

'Are we all agreeing that excellent communications with our customer base is essential?'

Next, chunk down, 'So we agree that improving communications between us will enhance the customer experience?' may be the point of agreement, and 'And how might we do that?' could move down another chunk. Notice 'how might we do that?', rather than 'how will we do that' gives choice and discussion in INVOLVE. The word 'will' implies there is only one way: remember the creation of options will lead to exploratory discussions and ultimately allow us move to the next chunk down, so the words 'may' or 'might' acknowledge that there are options and allows the next chunk down to emerge.

The skill and ability to chunk up and then slowly come down presents a real leadership challenge. Our observations of behaviours in organisations is that people who know and understand the detailed nature of their business often look to resolve issues by adjusting or changing those details *before* having gained agreement as to the principles or concepts of what it is they are trying to achieve.

By chunking up, and then allowing the process to come downwards towards detail, alternative and more creative solutions appear.

Chunking can help if you:

- Find yourself stuck in a negotiation or argument and are not able to find areas of agreement.
- Feel overwhelmed by the amount of activity.
- Need to quickly and easily think laterally.
- Seek to get something done, yet do not feel excited about it.
- Find it hard to get shared responsibility and a sense of what 'we' can do about it.

Language is important in chunking.

When you chunk up you become less detailed:

Good questions you may ask include . . .	**Or you might say . . .**
• What is this an example of?	This is an example of . . .
• What is this a part of?	This is part of . . .
• What is the intention?	The intention behind this is to . . .
• What is its purpose?	The purpose of this is to . . .

These are BIGGER questions and deliver more general information, background and context by taking discussions upward.

To chunk down gets into more detail:

Good questions you may ask include	**Or you might say . . .**
What is an example of this?	An example of this might be . . .
What is a component/part of this?	Part of this would be . . .
What/who/where specifically?	Jane could be involved on Mondays . . .
How might you do this?	It could be achieved by . . .

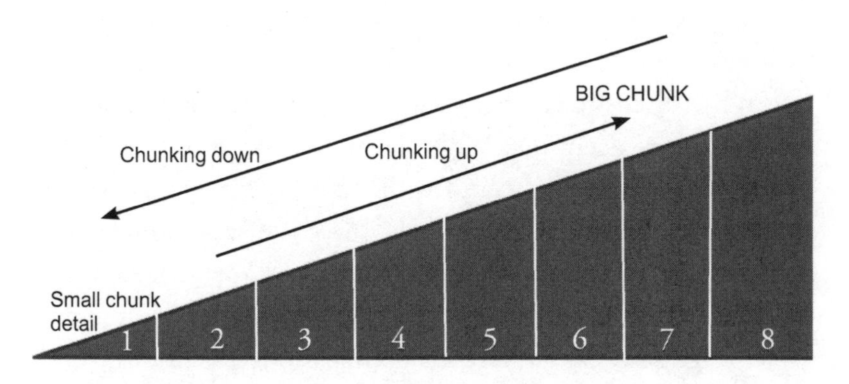

Using this sliding scale, let's look at an example.

While working with an organisation that was rebranding, a crucial meeting was rapidly heading towards conflict, as they discussed where they would best use their new logo and brand to full effect (mid chunk 4).

It needed a swift intervention to chunk up and move them up by asking a question about just what look and feel they wanted to project as a company: 'What is an important example about the values of your company?' 'Listening and responding to our customers' individual needs' was the reply, and all agreed on that big chunk statement (chunk 8)

But once again, they plunged into the detail and started

to disagree as to where to focus on using their logo, and again had to be chunked up.

By asking, 'What kind of design might portray listening and responding to your customers?', the responses included: 'Warm, friendly, approachable, natural, caring, sturdy, and reliable'. This could then be followed up with: 'And what kind of colours, solid, blue, green, earth etc?' (chunk 7)

So then they were asked, 'What best symbolises those values?' After much deliberation they decided that the large oak in the centre of their company gardens best captured what they were about (chunk 6): sturdy, reliable, natural, and healthy.

The discussions went on chunking slowly downwards towards the detail that had to be agreed, yet at a pace that everyone could follow and with little disagreement. 'And what would be an example of the sorts of places you would like to be associated with, that match your principles and company values?' (chunk 5). Examples poured forth, most were agreed to, although some were a little contentious, yet all were talked through, in the context of their company values, and in a good atmosphere given the earlier higher levels of agreement.

'And so specifically, let's look as some examples of where you might market their business' (chunk 4): again a range of suggestions emerged.

'Where and what methods might be deployed to achieve this?' (chunk 3): the detail continued to emerge effortlessly.

Now the meeting could get into real detail, that was meaningful to all, and look to PRODUCE a set of actions that would achieve agreed goals. A detailed implementation plan that included merchandise ideas to purchase and commission various products, etc, was produced with ease (chunk 2), and the plans for timescales, reporting methods and allocation of tasks (chunk 1) were all completed within the meeting.

The very practical value of chunking is that a solution to a problem becomes 'our solution' and we can move to PRODUCE by determining what we need to do and how we might achieve that. In this simple example as soon as any discord appeared in the group the process chunked up to the last point of agreement and down again. In reality there was little disagreement, and as they chunked down from their values it became obvious to all what was and was not appropriate.

Notice how many meetings you go to that start in the detail and therefore start in conflict. Chunking up saves time and energy: always start at the top and work down. Even if all the principles are already agreed, it's a great place to start as talking detail is so much easier with a team that are already nodding at points that have previously been agreed. So it's time well spent.

Principles of Negotiating in INVOLVE

When a leader knows that he or she is going to have to negotiate, then there are certain principles that are helpful:

- Prepare for the negotiation
  - There is an old adage: it is 90% preparation and 10% negotiation. Hence 'winging it' is usually unwise!
- Be prepared to accept other 'alternative best solutions'.
- Be prepared to use 'chunking' to find the start point of agreement.

Next, you need to decide what you want to achieve. This includes:

- What do you want?
- What do you NOT want?

It is important that you can answer both questions. Obvious, you may think, yet experience informs us that people usually have a stronger feeling as to what they want, or what they don't want, and understand that point better, and therefore will be able to cover it in greater detail. For example, if someone is opposed to a course of action, they would more readily be able to state just what it is they don't want to see happen, explaining in detail why. But when asked what they do want, it is usual to expect a short, brief, and less thought-through response. Try it the other way around, assume you have your VISION, real clarity about what you want, why you want it, what the benefits would be, what needs to happen, and so on, yet when asked what you don't want, is the answer as comprehensive? Usually not, it is often a summary statement like, 'not to carry on as it is'.

To be an empowered and skilled influencer you must have a comprehensive knowledge both of what you want and what you don't want. Why?

- You may find yourself in a polarised position with no flexibility to move even the slightest way. If all you know is what you want, you have already constructed your arguments, and are not in a flexible position to negotiate.
- It's hard to explore settlement ranges if you don't know what the ends of the scale are (see below).
- Everything is in danger of becoming your bottom line and not negotiable. If it is not negotiable, YOU CAN'T NEGOTIATE.
- You may not have previously considered something that legitimately undermines or discredits your position; someone may think of a good reason why some-

thing should not happen, and if you only have one position, with no place to move, it is very disabling.

So, exclusively knowing exactly what you want, in a strange way, can work against you when influencing others.

This gives us the concept of the settlement range:

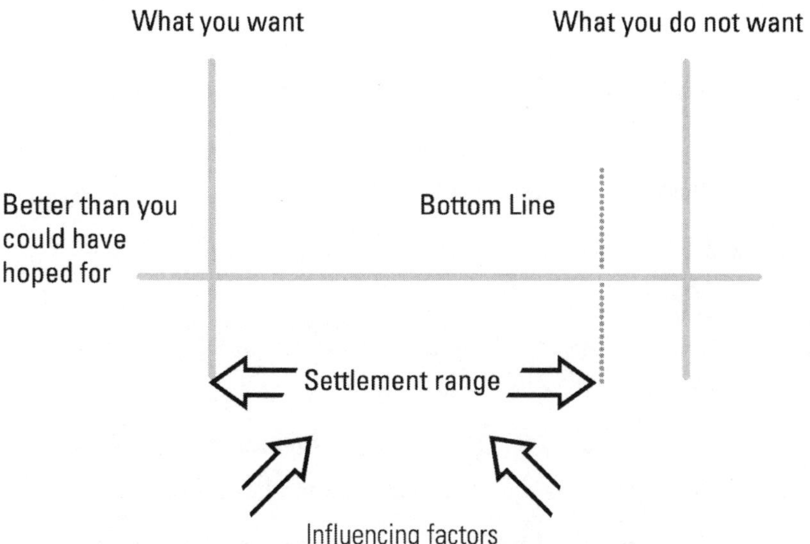

This diagram implies that it is mandatory to decide what your 'bottom line' is. This can be variably closer to 'what you do not want', depending on how much movement you believe there could be. However, it does represent the limit beyond which you will not negotiate.

By understanding the settlement range in negotiating, you can start to see where there is room for movement and where agreements can be settled.

To further understand the settlement range, it is often useful to see how a PEST analysis, or as it was later developed, a PESTLE analysis, influences matters by considering the settlement from three perspectives.

1. From your own perspective
2. From the perspective of the other party
3. From a neutral, detached perspective

Political – Is there a large political force at play here that is forcing the hands of you or the other party?

Economic – can you afford to do this or not – what is the financial impact on both parties?

Social – Is public opinion on your side, is this wanted or opposed?

Technological – Do you have the technology to be able to achieve this?

Legal – Are there any legalities or legislation that could prevent you or the other party undertaking this?

Environmental – Are there any environmental issues or others that may restrict or prevent progress? What corporate 'sustainability' matters need to be taken into account?

These PESTLE factors should also be considered in relation to the impact they have on each other. All this intelligence will allow you to adjust expectations and set realistic, achievable points of negotiation.

So putting this together, you may choose to have a list of what you want and what you don't want, with an understanding of all the issues from the differing perspectives. Now look down the list and notice just what movement there could be on each issue and where your bottom line is for each aspect. Having done this, you are in a pretty empowered place to commence your negotiation.

It is important to note that, as you enter your discussions, your bottom line is purely for you to be aware of, and not to be disclosed, until it absolutely needs to be. Do not be tempted to say something is your bottom line when you know it isn't. If you declare a bottom line, and then move from it, you have disabled yourself for any future negotiation, you don't 'mean what you say'.

So for example:

What you want	**What you don't want**
Task completed in 2 months	Completed by month 5
To produce 12 units per week	To produce less than 9 units per week
One lead responsible person	No junior or second in command
Meet defined high spec standards	Just to meet industry standards

In addition, there is one 'do' and one 'do not':

- The 'do' is to talk about 'points of agreement'.
  People like to achieve things and be thanked, so 'thanks, I'm pleased we were able to reach an agreement' has real strength.
- The 'do not' is not to talk about 'compromise'. Compromise can be interpreted by both sides as losing.

People don't like to be 'compromised' so if at the end of a well-constructed piece of negotiation you announce 'thanks for making that compromise' or 'I'm glad we have been able to make a compromise'– ouch, you have just taken something away from the impact: it sounds and feels like a loss rather than a gain.

When asking people, buying a product, to rank the elements of trust, cost and right product, in order of importance, they often say:

1st: Price – I want to pay the right amount and have a ceiling, and won't pay more.

2nd: Right product – I need it to do what I want

3rd: Trust – I need to trust the person selling it to me

Startlingly, quite the opposite is the case. Dr. Chester L. Karrass is the author of five books on negotiation, including *The Negotiating Game*.

Work undertaken within the field of negotiation indicated something quite different and established that the weighting of influence is as follows:

1st: Strength of relationship 56% (do I trust this person?)

2nd: Right product 38% (does this do what I need to do?)

3rd: Price 6% (cost)

This means that when you have the right rapport and relationship in place, whether that is with a colleague, employee or customer the percentage chance of success increases significantly. Obvious, you might say, yet when preparing to negotiate or influence others where is the majority of attention placed?

Our healthy negotiation equation works like this

Good relationship and rapport (trust)

+

Alternative best solutions (exploration & choice)

=

Agreed right solution at right price

So, if the leader spends time getting a good, genuine rapport there is an increased opportunity to create trust. Having done so, the leader can then describe in full glory the VISION and create the environment to gain the commitment required to become INVOLVED

Now it is time to 'negotiate' as to how to go about PRODUCING the outcome and this is where choice/alternatives can be introduced. 'So we could achieve this by doing X, Y or Z, what do you think?' By introducing realistic options, you are shifting the discussion to more greatly INVOLVE the other person in exploring the choices, and gaining their involvement in the outcome.

In addition, by offering choice you fundamentally shift the discussion by taking the focus away from, 'Should I do this?', or 'Do I want this or not?', which is a problem when faced with no options, to, 'Which of these do I think is the best way?' or 'Right solution?', hence promoting choice.

Far too often we observe people and organisations placing a great deal of effort in identifying what they want of others, or what their fixed price is, however the lack of investment in establishing a good rapport leads to:

Finding the right solution

+

Identifying the best price or best actions to be taken

=

Failure to agree

Although often done with all the best intentions, a combination of the lack of investment in building rapport and an eagerness to find the right solution and to secure the best price, interrupts or bypasses the process of building trust, which is the essential component to gaining real commitment (INVOLVE).

Great visions are designed and constructed, that then need a wide variety of people and professions to be INVOLVED, often including those outside any line management authority. Without proper rapport, it is therefore frustrating to see how much energy goes to waste and to hear: 'We worked out the problem, discovered a great solution, made it as cost-effective as we possibly could, and still they don't agree.'

So when looking to INVOLVE others, what possible options could you create? The creation of good alternatives can shift people's mindsets, moving from 'do I agree with how this is going to be done?', to 'which way do I think is the best way to do it, out of these options?'. Now people are involved, you have invited them to explore opinions over the best direction to take. The danger often is that if you own the VISION, you have probably thought it through in detail, when others have not. Bear in mind that the greater the detail at the outset of engaging others, with the VISION and then INVOLVE, the greater the possibility of conflict or disagreement. It is always important to start discussion from a constructive point of agreement, at the earliest possible time.

Matching – Pacing – Leading in INVOLVE

MATCHING, PACING AND LEADING IS PERHAPS a slightly surprising, and for some people a worrying concept. Nevertheless, there is a sufficient volume of information to show that this is a useful process. In this process, you are reflecting the person with whom you are communicating, reflecting their physical position, and the pitch, tone and pace of their speech.

If you are in good rapport with those you are influencing, it is hardly noticeable, in fact it is so subtle that it is 'natural'. If you observe close friends talking, unconsciously they start to reflect each other's body language, they talk at a similar pace, and they nod together, laugh together and the conversations flows back and forth seemingly effortlessly.

Often when influencing others there may not be the same established level of friendship. This coupled with some tension, perhaps because the person is sceptical about your 'big idea' and has not yet bought into becoming INVOLVED, resulting in you being tested as the leader who has to prove to them the worth of what you are proposing. You must have a well-constructed reason (VISION) and hold the evidence to support your position. Remember at this point the findings of Albert Mehrabian, in others words 'it ain't what you say, it's the way that you say it'.

So setting the scene, your sceptic is sitting back in a chair, calm, quiet, relaxed and still waiting to hear your story. You arrive, excited by the opportunity ahead, motivated and passionate, and displaying the immense energy of the enthused leader. Sitting opposite them, upright in your chair, as you initiate your discussion by describing the motives and delivering your evidence, your hands are creating shapes, your arms open as if physically embracing your ideas, you speak fast: you can't tell them quick enough. STOP, you are out of rapport, what is the person opposite you thinking?

Setting the alternative scene of a small team of staff standing in their office laughing, one just back from a fabulous holiday catching up on how things have been, expecting their leader to enter the room, at any point, to tell them about an exciting new contract the company has just been awarded that could create some real opportunities for them: the noise level and energy are high. You, the leader, arrive calm and measured. You take a seat and, speaking quietly, take them through the news of the new contract, and sitting quite still, you explain in a soft consistent voice how exciting this opportunity is. STOP. You are out of rapport, what are they thinking?

We recall one senior manager, known to us some years ago, who had one style, one approach. It was amusing to overhear another senior leader capture his impact on his arrival to any business environment with acute precision, as she declared 'when he enters the room it is as if eleven people just left'.

ISN'T IT GREAT THAT WE REALLY COMMUNICATE?

Matching the person or people is an important aspect of having your message not just heard, but received and understood; after all it is not the delivery of the message that is important, it is how it is received. Consider the real-life example of a conference where the industry was in an unpredicted and unprecedented downturn, redundancies imminent and many an individual contemplating deeply both their company's and their own future. On walks the motivational speaker, bounding with energy like some adult children's entertainer: 'Hey guys what I want to talk to about for the next 45 minutes is PMT' [smile/grin], 'Positive Mental Thoughts'. [Slaps hands together and skips towards front of stage.] Most of the audience are wishing that they were in possession of a high-calibre rifle.

You may think we have given some rather outrageous examples to make the point, yet this happens at a micro level: slight changes in how you interact may have a huge impact on the reception of your message. So it is important to match the energy in the room, or of the other person, and stay with it, then, when in good rapport, influence it yourself by taking the lead and changing the state (see below).

Matching

Matching is the process of establishing a physical likeness (posture not looks) and mirroring the pitch, tone, volume and pace of the interaction. It is worth noting here that by mirroring we do not mean mimicking, which is a sure way to receive another poke in the eye. Yet by reflecting even 50% of each party's physicality you can have a huge impact on rapport. Reflecting back, hands, arms, and head movements, can be a real challenge for you to learn, and at first could feel uncomfortable. Go with it, and if you do this with absolute integrity, you can build that all-important rapport you need as a leader: it will make all the difference.

Pacing

Pacing is the process of gracefully mirroring and moving in response to the other person over a sustained period of time, thus enabling rapport to be established. Note again, that this does not warrant you moving in synchrony with the other party. This would too quickly be detected by the other party, and create highly undesirable results.

With a self-assured poise, pacing the person allows you to continue to match your physical posture to reflect that of the other person. Likewise, adjust the pace of your speech, volume, pitch and tone, being careful not to mimic and keeping the process full of integrity.

Leading

Leading naturally follows from effective matching and pacing. Indeed, with experience there comes an unconscious point where sufficient rapport has been developed so that you, the leader, are able to slowly adjust the pace and energy you require, slowing down or speeding up, gaining volume or quietening off, so that others will often automatically and unconsciously follow your lead. Now you can start to really emphasise the points you wish to make while in genuine rapport, gaining approval and commitment of others.

When talking people through this technique they often say 'Oh yes, I've just realised I do that with many colleagues, customers and others', and you may well. What about those you find 'hard work', or who are senior to you, or those who try to 'intimidate you'? Just as rapport can unconsciously be established, it can easily be unconsciously broken and that is probably when you need it the most.

It does throw some traditional approaches out of the window, when what was often advocated was a calm, constant, quiet exterior to whatever you were faced with, be it the angry customer shouting, or the withdrawn employee who is hard to engage with.

- If the person is angry, raise your voice towards the loudness of their speech (careful not to shout back), nod, give them good eye contact, enter the discussion, hold that state and then after some time, quieten your voice, slow down your speech and movement, and then sit down.
- If they are withdrawn and talking slowly, match their posture and speed, slow down to their speed, and

then, as you start to explore the solution, quicken your speech and, by adding some energy, pull them in.

From pacing, you can move to rapport with the individual and then you are leading him or her towards a communication state that makes INVOLVE an easier process.

Asserting Yourself in INVOLVE

MANY LEADERS HAVE DIFFICULTY STRIKING THE right amount of assertiveness, according to a study in the February 2007 issue of the *Journal of Personality and Social Psychology*, published by the American Psychological Association. It found that being under-assertive or over-assertive may be the most common weakness among aspiring leaders.

It is always interesting to ask people to rate their perception of their own assertiveness as in the scale in the diagram on page 167, and then ask others around them and note the difference. As a leader, knowing when to assert a point of view, an action or an approach that you don't want to see adopted is an important ability and an early appropriately placed assertion can save much later distress and reduce any misunderstanding. Being consistently assertive does not mean that you stop listening. Assertion is not about being difficult, it is about providing clarity.

At one end of the scale is the non-assertive individual perceived as timid, weak, even vulnerable, and at the other end, the aggressive individual perceived as single-minded, a bully who controls by fear. In practice, the negotiation zone lies around assertive behaviour, within which it is possible to communicate with those around you with consistent lucidity. If your leadership swings like a pendulum between non-assertion and aggression, then those around you will watch and wonder, and will hesitate to join you in INVOLVE.

The pendulum effect does happen and is characterised by a non assertive person bottling up what they wanted to assert, holding it in for fear of offending or generating a response they would then have to deal with. Ultimately though, 'pop', the bottle bursts, and out pours what was meant to be said, and often much more besides, and in an emotionally powered way that is at best unhelpful and at worst extremely damaging.

Alternatively the aggressive person increases their aggression at times of frustration, building to a crescendo, and again 'pops'. Those with insight may realise they have gone too far and grovellingly have to apologise, while others may only find out when legal or other company internal procedures are taken out against them. Whichever the consequences, it is ultimately humiliating, disempowering and damaging to any leadership aspirations, taking away power and ultimately the ability realistically to assert.

Think of those really influential people across the world, those who have impact and who change things: their composure is often everything. They use the time to sit back, make eye contact and talk in a calm, clear manner, without the need to overly raise the volume of their voice, just delivering a well-timed, well-balanced assertion that all hear and understand. Assertiveness is nothing about raising your voice or wagging your finger, it is all about calmness and clarity, espe-

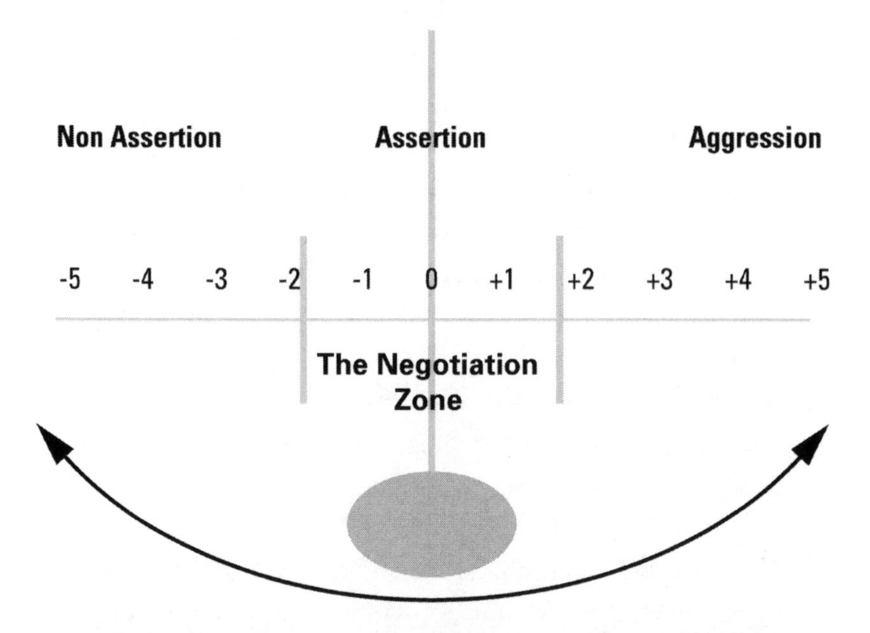

cially when times are challenging or high pressure: difficult times do not require difficult people with difficult behaviours.

When negotiating a change in behaviour, there is a very useful six-point tool that helps deliver information with authority, creates a real presence for the leader and has an impact on the recipient:

1. Objective description of the individual's behaviour.
2. The effect that has, and how you feel about it.
3. The bigger consequence of the behaviour, for example on the company.

Chunk up to the point of agreement

4. Description of preferred ' new behaviour'.
5. The effect that would have, and how you would feel about that.

6. The bigger consequences of the new behaviour on everyone.

When having to be assertive with underperforming individuals, try not to get involved in discussions with yourself about whether you should use a soft or hard approach; try a clear, unambiguous one. If they know they are underperforming and have insight, the person's level of anxiety is already likely to be sky-high and so the soft, small-talk approach while they wait for the bad news to emerge is cruel. However the hard approach of straight away telling them what you think about them, together with everything that is wrong, will result in the person either not hearing the real message because they become scared, or becoming angry and want to defend themselves and respond to your 'accusations': either way it is not constructive.

Once you've told them that you want to discuss a difficult topic, move right in to the topic and use the following steps:

1. **Objective description – specific facts that cannot be disputed and delivered dispassionately without any comment**
   Last Wednesday when you were expected to arrive at 9 to open the office you didn't arrive until 9.45.'

2. **The effect, its immediate impact, and how you felt**
   This delayed our ability to make the decision within the same working day and therefore delayed our customer response time, losing that customer's faith in us and leaving me disappointed and frustrated that we were unable to achieve this.'

3. **The bigger consequences**
   'This ultimately gives the advantage to our competitors who were able to respond much quicker. Also, if this customer decides to speak to others, this could damage our reputation.'

Now CHUNK UP – big statement all will agree with –
'The stability and future of the company is paramount for all our futures', or,' my vision is for this company to grow and be one of the leading providers across the country'.

4. **The preferred alternative**
   'It is therefore imperative that in future you ensure the office is open and functioning for our advertised opening time of 9 a.m.'

5. **The effect**
   'This would ensure we met the needs of our customer and kept their loyalty to our brand.'

6. **The consequence**
   'Ensuring this does not happen again leaves us in a good position to protect our reputation in the market and ensure that we continue to grow and meet our development aspirations.'

When reading this you may find it too simple even to imagine you could do this. Observing people, they tend to miss out much of this process. Just focusing on negatives and what has gone wrong can be a real problem. So, just stating what is wrong and that 'something needs to be done about it' or 'I don't want that to happen again' is not helpful, can even be counterproductive, and does not result in solutions that will allow the organisation to move into PRODUCE.

Customer services model

When seeking to INVOLVE those around you to PRODUCE, it is useful to reflect on how your attitude and behaviour are likely to influence others. This model is taught to those in the service industries and illustrates how to deal with difficult customers.

This model is useful, and we can all recognise ourselves in this diagram – the classic vicious circle:

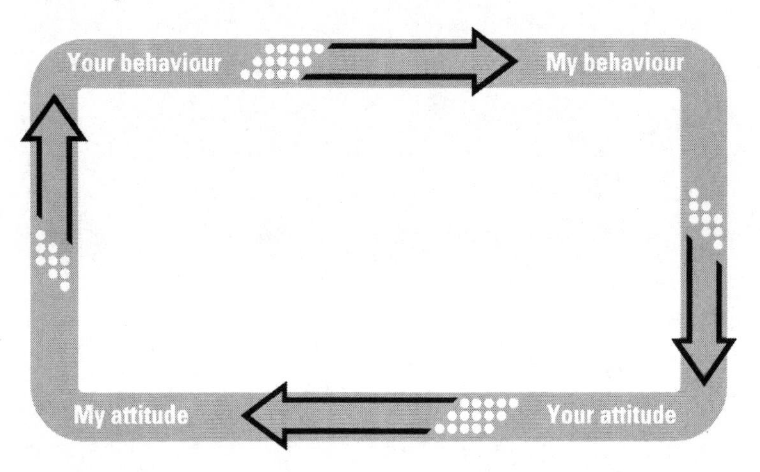

What we think on the inside leaks out, therefore our attitude directly affects our behaviour, subtle or not. Our behaviour in turn affects the attitude of others, both towards us and the task we have to complete, and again, in turn, affects their behaviour.

As we have said, this is a classic vicious circle which may well result in any argument:

- Becoming more heated
- Leading to worsening insults
- Possibly even becoming aggressive or violent

The message for your behaviour, as leader, is clear and perhaps on this occasion we should refer back to the three ego states described in transactional analysis. As the leader we need to be in the adult ego state, synthesising the facts and making logical, rational statements rather than using or falling into the more emotive parent or child states. We cannot deny that our attitudes affect our behaviours, so the challenge to the leader is to constantly check out attitudes, as they change and adapt to others and changing situations. How helpful is your attitude towards others, and what you are trying to achieve?

We hope now that, using your innate skills as a leader, and possibly modified by our suggestions, that your team have completed the INVOLVE phase and are committed and ready to PRODUCE.

PRODUCE

Principles of PRODUCE

As we said right at the beginning of this book, we considered using the word 'perform'or even 'performance', yet at its simplest leadership produces something whether that be a product, a concept or a change in attitude, or a perception. So we use the word PRODUCE in the context of bringing about something, overseeing the shape or form of something by intellectual or physical effort.

We do not want to get into the technicalities of production, as we want to explore the relationship that you, as the leader, have with those producing whatever the product or change that is required. How do you maintain inspiration and motivate others throughout the process? How do we push development areas while understanding how people react to changing environments, not forgetting to evaluate and learn from our various successes and failures?

Success will depend on your attention to each component of the VIP process:

- That the VISION continues to be shared by the team.
- That INVOLVE includes the right people and that they remain wholehearted and committed, and that the team is being developed through healthy working relationships and by development of their individual leadership skills.
- That VISION and INVOLVE are being regularly reviewed and reflected upon through PRODUCE.

Good Communication in PRODUCE

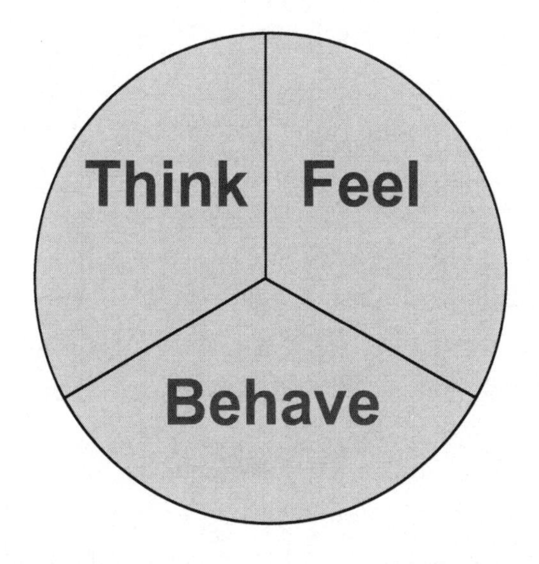

GOOD COMMUNICATION IS EVERYTHING IN PRODUCE. We have focused a lot on the need for excellence in communication and believe that often the simplest of models can give us great insight. As the diagram shows, the Mercedes Model gets its name from the iconic symbol of the Mercedes car and was developed in this format by Bandler and Grinder, the early pioneers of Neuro Linguistic Programming (NLP). The Mercedes Model taps into everything that makes us function and it is important for the leader to use it, because of the insights it gives us. The interesting thing about this model is that, whenever we change one aspect, we automatically start to alter the other two, so for example if I change what I'm doing, it will affect how I feel and what I think.

Internal Processing –THINKING

Processing our internal thoughts, the things we say to ourselves about what is happening around us, or how we have VISION and picture things in our mind. These thoughts can also start to create our understandings and beliefs about ourselves and the wider world.

Internal Emotions – FEELING

We translate the sensations and feelings we experience into emotions and in turn we use our emotions to start to create our values of 'how we feel' about things.

External Behaviours – DOING (behave)

Actions, including, movements, body gestures, eye movements, facial expressions and even breathing make up external behaviours.

If you are alive in the world today you are at all times Thinking, Feeling and Behaving. It is important that the leader accesses each aspect and therefore has clarity about their own thoughts, feelings and behaviours and an understanding of other people's.

One observation from coaching prompts us to ask the question, 'Could it be possible that, certainly when it comes to communicating with others, we put more emphasis on two of think, feel or behave, and ignore or rather neglect one or other?'

The reason for asking is that our experience leads us to suggest that when articulating information to others there is not one dominant one, but more often one weaker one. We would invite you to notice, as people communicate, how their language is peppered with two of the three, and that one of the three elements is much less apparent:

Asking Questions or	Saying
What do you think?	Well I think that . . .
How does that feel?	I feel disappointed that . . .
What will you do about that?	I am going to do . . .

Could it be that there is one of these we use less conversationally or even hardly at all in our leadership communication with others? Some people tend to spend time talking about what they think and feel and much less about what they intend to do. Others talk dominantly about what needs to be done and what they think about that, much less how they feel about it. Then there are those who might talk about how they feel about what needs to be done, yet do not say what they really think about it.

In PRODUCE it is important for the leader to articulate all three elements:

Think – Feel – Behave

One of our former bosses, while highly respected and a good mentor, constantly enquired about what the person thought, seeking and valuing their opinion and frequently asking how they felt. Seldom did he ask what had been done, declaring things like 'How do you think it went at the board yesterday?' or 'Did you feel you got what you wanted from the meeting?' never, 'What did you do at the board or at the meeting to make it successful?' So although a competent leader, he constantly missed essential intelligence.

While working with groups of people and explaining the Mercedes Model it is not unusual for people to declare 'This is just common sense', or 'I do all three all the time', only to discover, on examination, that they do not. Indeed a finance director once declared, 'I do all those with my team', but then discovered from her colleagues that she rarely, if ever asked how people felt about things. This new information allowed her to add more emotion-based language into her interactions and she fundamentally adjusted her leadership style as she gained more insight and intelligence into the working of her department.

Let's do some test scenarios:

As the leader, you have proposed a change and the person is fairly supportive and having asked them what they think, you get the reply;

'Great idea, it should reduce inefficiency and make life easier in the process.'

'Great', you declare, 'and do you understand what to do?'

'Yes', comes the reply, 'we need to start moving from using this particular method to this way.'

'Fantastic, see you in two weeks.'

You leave confident the new approach will be adopted. Yet two weeks later, on your return you find that not to be the case, nothing has changed. Disappointed, you declare your frustration

'Why has this not happened, I thought we discussed it and you knew what to do and thought it a good idea?'

Before you go on lambasting them, STOP. What did you miss in your communication? What if you had additionally asked how they felt about doing it? 'Sorry, I think it's a great idea and know what to do, yet I haven't done this before, and I don't feel confident to do it for the first time, without instruction or guidance from someone more experienced.' Ah, new information that, if gathered at first, could have been resolved. Because they were not asked how they felt, no progress was made.

You can approach this for each of the components of the Mercedes model. 'I think it's great and feel relieved that the company have decided to change things this way.' Left at that, you could be under the impression things will happen, yet what if they 'don't know how to do it', oops, missed the behaviour out!

'I don't have any strong feeling about it and fully understand what you are asking us to do and I'm more than capable of doing it.' Great, see you in two weeks: oh no, task not done on your return! They happen to think it a silly way of doing it and have other more effective ideas, yet thoughts on the matter were not requested.

We would urge you not to fall into the trap of believing that asking people how they feel is somehow fluffy management speak. People are often governed by their feelings even if these feelings are not expressed. Often when people have a 'gut reaction' to something, it is not them simply being emotional, it is a whole host of experiences and knowledge that is telling them something is wrong, before they have had the opportunity to think it through or articulate their concerns.

Emotional Intelligence in Organisations

We see good use of the Mercedes model in organisations, and note how well organisations and their leadership understand the balance between what people think about working there, how they feel about working there, and how well they understand just what it is they are doing and the role they fulfil. All this is essential intelligence for anyone leading an organisation.

So it is important that the leader avoids the macho management world of tough business, where it is easy to slip into a tendency to enter the 'behave' sector, 'get on with it, and produce more, faster'.

We can, at times, observe organisations that go into action mode when there are plenty of tasks and lots to do. The danger is however that in this mode, organisations forget or neglect to understand what the workforce, or even customers, 'think' or 'feel'.

There are many examples of failed organisations that

were very busy failing, with myriad plans, projects, targets and lists of subsequent objectives. At worst, organisations that just enter into the behaviour mode of 'do more' can be in constant 'crisis management', becoming entirely reactive, rather than undertaking due process and using proactive planning through VIP.

The trap here is that once you stop asking, morale could well deteriorate, and the last thing you or your organisations will want to do is to ask what it feels like to work there, because you don't want to hear or acknowledge the answer you may get.

The Mercedes model is essential in all parts of the VIP process, although we have chosen to place it in the PRODUCE section, as it is vital to remember, when things start to happen, that the actions do not become everything. We can all be busy in any process, yet are we busy doing the right things, fully thinking things through, and does it feel right? Taking stock and reviewing think/feel/behave could be the difference between success and failure.

In your own leadership, it may be helpful repeatedly to ask yourself three questions:

- Are my own thoughts clear and positive?
- Are my feelings being expressed and am I articulating them appropriately?
- Are my own actions clear, and in line with what I think and feel?

Successful leaders, and indeed organisations, understand

and explore what people think, discover how people feel, and understand and inform behaviours.

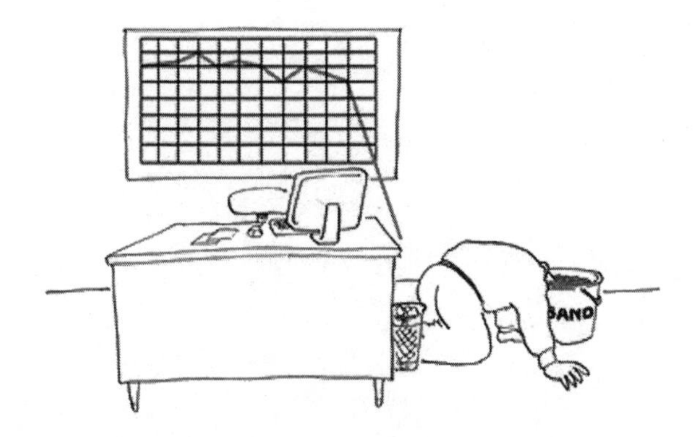

'Ah, the comfort of the office bucket'

Working Relationships in PRODUCE

YOUR WORKING RELATIONSHIP WITH THOSE AROUND YOU will need constant attention. We think it important to state a number of principles.

- It is not essential that you like those you work with. However, leading an effective team requires that there is mutual professional respect. So, it is important that you display respect and consideration for others at all times.
- Your relationships will need to be nurtured and where problems exist they need to be dealt with quickly and effectively. As the leader, you will need to act decisively to ensure good relationships exist, and that your behaviours are impeccable examples of what you expect from others.

- Show loyalty to those who are absent from the room or the immediate process, yet still very much part of it, and don't get embroiled talking or gossiping about others.
- Be visible with ongoing and open communication, let people see and hear you.
- Keep promises and follow through with anything you say you will do or undertake.
- Ensure competence in yourself, and then those producing will not tolerate incompetence.

Facilitating PRODUCE Using Logical Levels

It is important in PRODUCE that you keep momentum, and understand what continues to motivate and ensure that people will continue to produce to the standard and quality you wish. To enable us to understand this further, and keep PRODUCE on course, we look to the work of Robert Dilts.

Leading organisational change, or the adoption of new strategies, often requires people to change their behaviours. Leaders need to be aware that making adjustments to the way they are communicating and using the Logical Levels concept can help them to inspire and lead change.

This work allows us to understand the relationship between Environment, Behaviours, Skills and Abilities, Beliefs and Values, Identity and Purpose. By utilising this model, and ensuring an alignment between each aspect, a deeper understanding into motivation can be achieved.

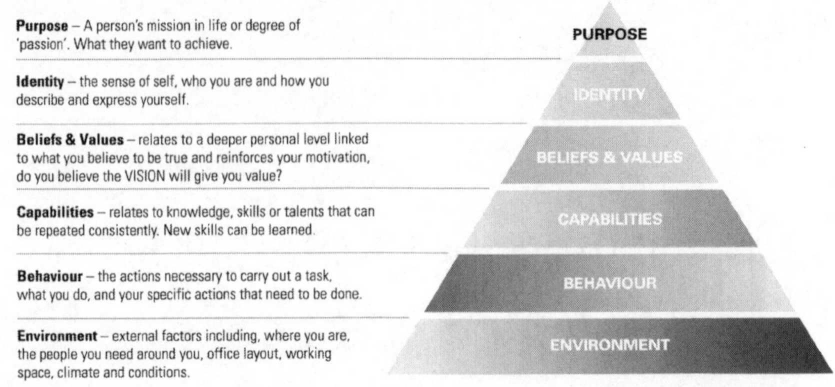

(c) Robert Dilts
Originally published in 'Changing Belief Systems with NLP' (1990).

- **Purpose** People with strong identity often give real meaning to what they PRODUCE. Knowing the purpose of PRODUCE may seem rather obvious; however, unless those around you feel it is worthwhile, they will not have this sense of purpose that drives VIP to its conclusion.
- **Identity** when the Logical Levels are in alignment it can lead to strong Identity and this is vital for each member of the team around you. You need to know each of them and their role in PRODUCE.
    - *One only has to look into society for examples of the impact of unemployment to see the effects of loss of identity, or in contrast, at professions to see the strong identities for example of a lawyer, doctor, or a teacher.*
- **Beliefs and values** When people believe something to be important to them they gain value and motivation, allowing the more effective use of their Skills and Abilities. This is a core part of INVOLVE.

- **Skills and abilities** when behaviours are right, and if the person has the correct skills available to them, then PRODUCE becomes possible.
- **Behaviours** will be strong and you will be doing 'the right thing' when the environment is correct.
- **Environment** is not only the physical environment but perhaps more importantly, it includes the relationships and the culture that have developed in that environment that will provide what we have described as 'the fertile ground' for PRODUCE.

The test of a good leader is to be able to articulate their vision through each of the Logical Levels starting from the higher purpose.

Working down the Pyramid, can you, the leader, describe the purpose (VISION), so that others can understand, a VISION that is aligned to, or helps create or give them an identity, and which they can then believe in, and will value undertaking? You will also need to ensure that the people have the skills and the abilities to undertake what it is they need to do, in an environment that is conducive to and supportive of everything they need to achieve in PRODUCE.

Logical Levels helps to further define the difference between managers and leaders. Managers place their focus at the bottom of the pyramid, on the physical environment, the equipment, and the performance of people. Whereas leaders need to have an awareness of the importance of aligning all elements, and focusing on and influencing people's beliefs and values, and the basic need people have for a sense of purpose in their lives, so they concentrate on the top of the pyramid.

When exploring problems, while in PRODUCE, if you come across things not happening don't just focus on behaviour. You can tell someone to do something hundreds of times but if they don't believe that it is important, it is likely either not to get done or not to be done to the standard that's needed.

As part of your exploration of behaviour, examine the level either side, that is, environment, and skills and abilities. So, if the required behaviour is not being displayed, ask yourself, 'Is the environment conducive to what I want someone to do? Or, do they have the skill and abilities to undertake what I am asking them to do?'. If you discover that they do have the ability, move upward: do they value what they are doing, and believe it to be important?

Leadership Within the Team in PRODUCE

Developing yourself

IT MAY NOW BE WORTH SPENDING SOME TIME TO REFLECT on the necessity of holding together the team around you. There are certain basic issues that we all need to accept in PRODUCE.

- As a leader, you cannot PRODUCE on your own.
- It is the team who will PRODUCE through VIP, even though you are the leader.
- Managers and leaders within the team who PRODUCE are vital.
- If the product is big, you will need to develop, inspire and allow others to lead in different components of PRODUCE.

Hence you will need to DELEGATE not just the task, also the authority. However, there are a number of questions you will want to ask yourself:

- Do they see the specific task as their job?
- If not, can you persuade them that it is reasonable for them to do it?
- Are they competent to do it? You may consider it unwise to delegate to someone who is not competent.

Inherent in delegation is the acceptance that the deals you have done have been completed in a clear way. Do you know?

- Who you have asked to do what?
- Did they agree to do it (Think)?
- Do they want to do it (Feel)?
- Do they know how to do it (Action)?

Do they have the skills to do it (Action)?

Developing others in your team

We've already said that, if the task is big in PRODUCE, then other members of the team will be leading in their areas within PRODUCE. Therefore it will be your responsibility to develop leadership in others. This will result in an improvement in the identity of all members of your team. The questions you could ask yourself are:

- Do others feel fulfilled?
- Are their ambitions being realised?
- Are their skills, and in this case their leadership skills, being utilised and developed?

In PRODUCE, the team needs to be able to demonstrate leadership in their individual spheres of responsibility.

The Road to PRODUCE

In VIP the start point, VISION, and the product must be clear, as must the endpoint, to ensure success in PRODUCE.

The diagram shows that there are, and will be, alternative roads to PRODUCE and empowering others to find the best road is the leader's task. Which prompts the question how do you define best? Best cost, best quality, best looking, best profile, best politically, the list could go on and on!

Yet the word 'best' is a generalisation often used. The leader needs to be so clear about just what is 'best', otherwise those following the leader will almost certainly be left to establish their own definition and unless possessed with advanced mindreading skills will almost certainly be working to completely different criteria of 'best'.

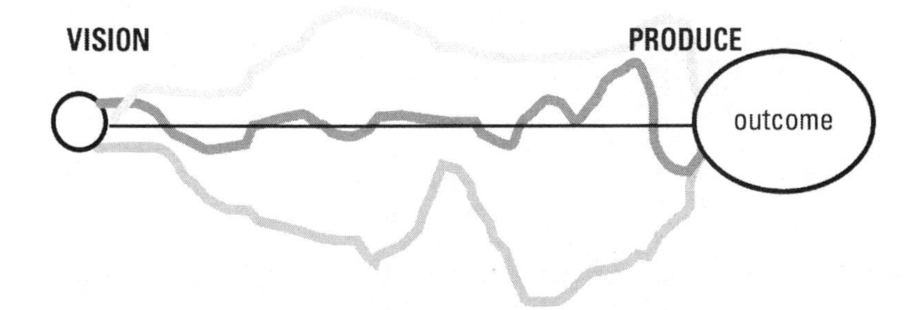

So, although the final VISION or outcome is likely to be non-negotiable, the road to achieve it may well be flexible, giving those in PRODUCE some choice as to the precise path they can take in order to reach the goal. This flexibility is essential, because in any stage of VIP, it can be necessary to revisit VISION and INVOLVE, and there may need to be changes to PRODUCE. Furthermore, the characteristics of the team may determine the precise route that you take and ensure they 'buy in' to the VISION final outcome.

Understanding Motivation

THERE ARE MANY THINGS THAT MOTIVATE PEOPLE. Maximising the internal motivation of the team in PRODUCE will smooth the path to completion by VIP. We want to explore two types of 'motivators' as motivation is the drive behind behaviour and intention. The two types we wish to explore in this book, and for the purpose of VIP, are called 'towards' motivators and 'away from' motivators:

- Towards Motivators
    - They want to do the task well, perhaps even better than is required
    - They may want to do the task faster than the required deadlines

- Away From Motivators
  - They do not want to fail
  - They may want to do it more thoroughly in order to make sure failure can't occur and the goal is achieved safely

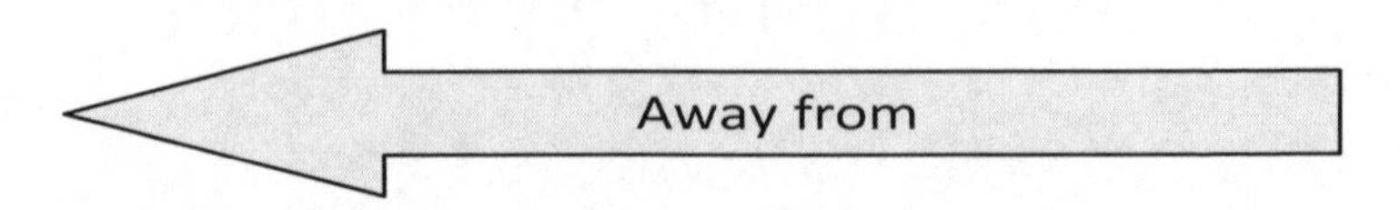

Both motivators can achieve results, and neither one nor the other is better or worse, the importance for the leader is to know when and how to tap into others' motivation, in order to in order to maximise the effectiveness of the PRODUCE process.

Recalling a studious 17-year-old, studying to ensure he achieved his grades to get into the university of his choice. He arranged a joint study time with his friend, a fellow student, every Sunday afternoon, where they jointly studied the Shakespeare plays required for their English examination. She arrived each week to undertake the task; on asking her motivation to be there, the response would be something like 'Oh, I want to get the best result I can so that my parents can be really pleased with my achievements', a clear 'towards motivator'. On turning to him, and making the same enquiry, the response would be something like 'Because I don't want to fail and miss out going to the university I want', a clear 'away from' motivator. So one was pushing for the best, and the other avoiding the worst, yet both achieved excellent end results and got to where they wanted to be. On the surface, it was not obvious which motivation was at play, but it was only by making the enquiry that the difference was identified. Then understanding the differentiation allowed the appropriate motivation to be applied, in order to support each of them in a way that best suited their type of motivation.

So he needed, 'Great to see you studying so hard, I'm sure this will ensure you don't fail and get the university experience you deserve' – smiles all round. It could have gone very differently if what was said was, 'Great to see you studying I'm confident this will ensure you get the best result you possibly can, and your mother and I will be so delighted': no smile on this occasion and we could have even just upped the pressure. He does not want to fail, so projecting a 'towards motivator' on to his 'away from motivator type' has not supported him in a way that registers with his preference.

She, on the other hand, needed 'Great, I'm sure your studying will make sure you get the best grades possible and indeed we'll all be very proud of you' – smiles all round. Yet to go against her motivator and say 'Great to see you studying, it will ensure you don't fail' – no smile. Not only no smile, but she is positively de-motivated by the comment as failure is not in her mind.

This gives us an important lesson that if we use the wrong type of motivators, even with the best of intentions, it is highly possible we may achieve just the opposite and de-motivate the individual.

It is quite common for people to enter the PRODUCE phase with 'away from' motivation 'Don't want to get it wrong' or 'I don't want to lose my job', only to switch along the way to 'towards' motivation as they become more energised and engaged.

It is important that, as the leader, you recognise which

motivator mode you are in, in any situation, before you start to identify and work with the motivation of others around you.

So the skill of a good leader is to notice which type of motivator he or she is, so that, when working with individuals, and when working with groups or teams, you can ensure that you support both types of motivators, as you can be fairly confident that any team will have both.

So in using both types of motivator we can delegate tasks appropriately and engage with the wider workforce:

> 'It is important we produce this to ensure that ours becomes the leading product in the market (use a towards motivator) and ensure the company does not slip behind (use an away from motivator) our competitors.'

or

> 'As we enter this next phase of achieving our VISION of becoming the most successful team in the corporation (towards), may I remind all of those INVOLVED of the importance in PRODUCING this outcome as, not achieving this (away from), would leave us bitterly disappointed, after all our concerted efforts: let's do it.'

Extreme 'towards' and 'away from' motivators:
Having said that both types of motivators can be positive and productive in PRODUCE, it is worth pointing out that you may come across people who are extreme, very 'towards' or very 'away from'. At the extremes, both types can be problematic for the leader.

'Away from' can:	'Towards' can:
• Become too worried about failure • Be too risk averse • Want to check and test things more than necessary • Slow down progress • Lose sight of the VISION and get lost in detail	• Be too focused on the outcome • Stop listening to others • Become unaware of the chaos they cause in their wake • Be perceived by others as bullies

Anyone with experience of working with others, in any industry, will no doubt recognise both these extremes; yes they are there and have the potential to make life a little harder than it need be. It is worth asking yourself where others will place you, are you part of the problem, does your enthusiasm and commitment mean you are an extreme towards motivator?

The two types of motivators need to be led in different ways.

Though the principal is easy, putting it into practice takes some careful thought; it is based around meeting them, by going in the same direction and influencing them by being in tune with their understanding of the world around them, and not yours.

Firstly, 'towards' motivators:

'Go with them' is the principal message.

To create a test scenario we will assume that you are

working with an extreme 'towards' motivator. They are rushing off creating ambitious (if not impossible) deadlines and you wish to rein them in, without de-motivating them, and get them to reconsider whether their timescales are realistic.

Go with their motivation, 'I understand you want to achieve this in the next six weeks.'

And then build on it, 'AND, how can I help you achieve your objective?'

Adding your motivation and any requirements, 'whilst ensuring that we . . .' Now introduce your other concerns or motives, whether it is keeping within budget, ensuring safety and so on. You need to rein them in by gently asking them to face the practicalities of the situation.

Notice the **' . . . AND, how can I . . . '**

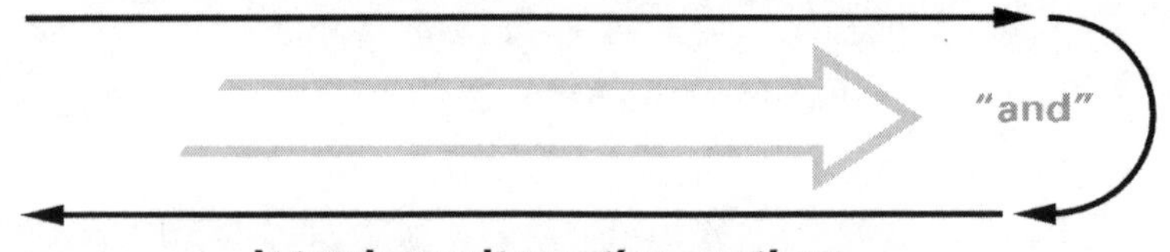

We spoke earlier about how poor we are at handling negatives. The temptation when trying to rein back the forward motivators is to say 'Yes, but . . . ' or 'Ah, however . . . '. To the forward motivator, let's be really clear about this, 'Yes, but . . . ' or 'however' means NO and the 'towards' motivated person will then tend to switch off, ignore you or maybe not even hear what you are saying.

When dealing with the 'forward motivators', it is important not to be disingenuous in your replies and to keep them properly involved in PRODUCE and therefore 'on board'. As we've said, you must acknowledge where they are in their thought processes. However, it is important to:

- Agree when you see no problem.
- Do not agree when you clearly do see a problem.
- Always acknowledge their wishes by making reference to them without necessarily accommodating them.
- If you have to disagree because there is a clear problem, chunk up to achieve a new point of agreement.
- Try to get them to question whether their road to PRODUCE is as effective as it could be.

The 'away from' motivator needs to be handled differently, yet using similar principles:

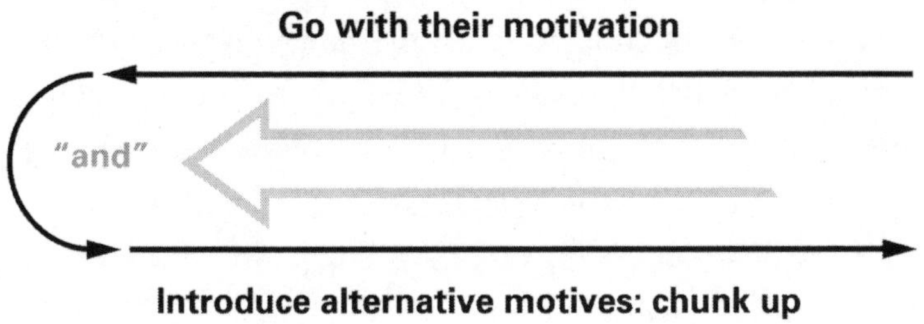

Go with their motivation

"and"

Introduce alternative motives: chunk up

Go with their motivation, 'I understand you have concerns about whether this can be achieved within the next six weeks?'

And then build on it, 'AND, how can I help address your

concerns?'

By adding your motivation or requirements, 'while ensuring we stay on course for this deadline, and keeping in cost, ensuring safety . . .' and so on, you are once again reining them in to face realities.

Chunk up – 'this is an important part of the company's current aspirations and its success will allow us to go on and thrive.'

- Acknowledge their concerns
- Suggest ways that PRODUCE can be speeded up, perhaps by saying 'Can we work together to look at the time frame?'

The danger with extreme 'away from' motivators is that they can suffer from 'paralysis from analysis', so, they may need extra reassurance and support.

Furthermore, what is also vital is that, in leadership, we give very clear answers, so 'Yes' and 'No' are clear; however 'Yes, but...' is not clear. So it is important to replace the 'but' with an 'and', therefore saying, 'Yes, and . . . The 'and' allows you to sound more supportive rather than a dismissive 'but'. It also enables you to build on what has been said rather than shutting down or closing off others' suggestion. Importantly, the use of 'and' will contribute to you retaining the attention of those with 'towards' motivators, so you can then ask him or her detailed questions as to how they can achieve their (overambitious) timeline.

Pushing Development Boundaries

Expanding the team's comfort zone in PRODUCE

THIS GIVES A VERY CLEAR INDICATION OF HOW TO approach the development of the team members during PRODUCE, and it will apply not only you as the leader, but also to all members of the team around you. It works on an individual and organisational level, and will increase the efficiency of your VIP process.

The area in which people perform well and want to be is the Comfort Zone, which is hopefully the segment in the diagram that describes tasks that are needed and which we are good at. However, in PRODUCE, we often have to expand our 'Comfort Zone', towards the things we do less well but are very much needed. The leader needs to be aware that, even though there are areas where there are needs which must be met, if we do not feel comfortable doing those particular tasks, many of us will try to avoid them. We could at this point get all macho and talk about the importance of individuals and organisations needing to work outside their comfort zone, however most humans, unless they have some form of fetish (lying on a bed of nails), seek comfort in life, and therefore do not like to be uncomfortable. To suddenly push people out of their comfort zone is too stressful for many and leads to a 'sink or swim' position. So, if you are the leader who relishes that 'new zone' and wants to push there too quickly, just remember it is unlikely that your followers will always share your enthusiasm.

So, the skill here is to get your teams working at their best within their comfort zone and yet accustomed to continuously pushing down to expand their comfort zone in achievable amounts. This may sound like just playing with words, yet remember 'words matter' and as the leader you must use them wisely. All tasks have to be completed, and so it is the task of the leader to align the capabilities of the team with the tasks to be completed to ensure PRODUCE.

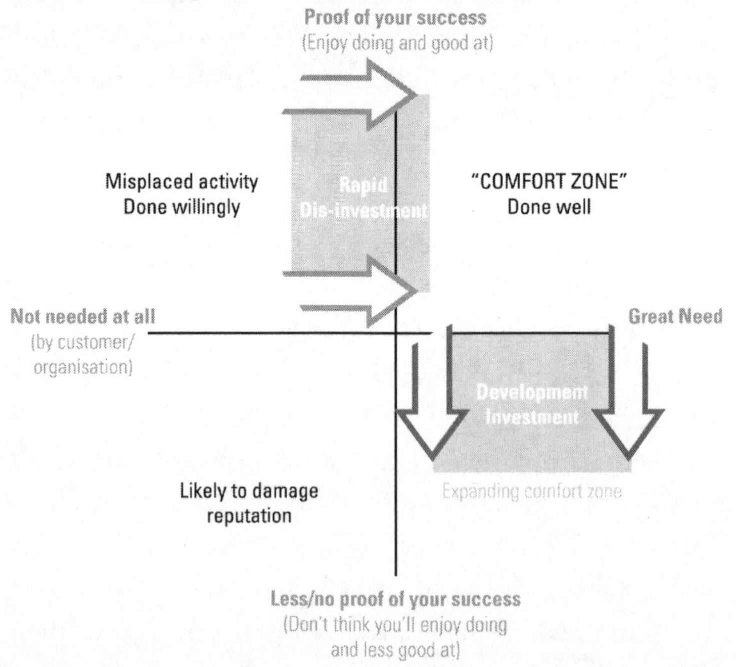

As leader, it will be important that development tools are made available that allow both you and your team to expand your Comfort Zone, whether through, training, coaching, mentoring, shadowing, or secondments.

The tendency to work within our comfort zone has another down side. What if the tasks you are good at are no longer needed? Another danger is that when under stress, or when tired, when not stretched, or when not stimulated, we can tend to drift across into doing things that we are good at but are not needed. Working in companies and organisations going through significant change, we have witnessed a great deal of misplaced activity, with people doing what they are good at, but not doing what is really needed. Perhaps this is to subconsciously somehow justify their existence; prove their worth to the system, and to show how competent they are. What we suggest is that people and organisations, naturally and unconsciously, drift in this unproductive direction whereas for PRODUCE it is necessary to focus on 'what needs to be done' and either develop the skills of the team in order to carry out these tasks, or find those who can.

The big question is who is defining what is needed and giving direction; it should be you, 'the leader', yet in large, complex organisations you may feel it is not. Step up to the mark and start to define for others just what is needed, own this responsibility; it is a key leadership issue.

Drifting into misplaced activity can happen with people and companies that overspecialise and can't or won't change with the times, such as Kodak. Working in healthcare we have noticed those skilled surgeons who have been very successful, even renowned at certain operative procedures, yet as time goes on, and new technology and procedures are introduced, either by choice or ignorance ignore the new technology and in time become outdated. They may end up sidelined, with people saying things like 'they were marvellous in their day'. Hence the acceptance of necessary change is vital in VIP, as it is in life.

Stepping back, the leader has to understand what is not needed and stop any team activities that will not help PRODUCE. This presents its own challenge as individuals may enjoy this activity or task, so all our techniques highlighted through the book will have to be deployed to keep these individuals 'onside'. We refer to this process as 'disinvestment', a term often associated with reduction in capital investment, yet here we define it in a much broader context, as those activities that need to be reduced or stopped altogether. This is disinvestment of time and energy going into unimportant areas, and transferring effort to areas of critical importance to PRODUCE.

Once identified, it is important to disinvest rapidly, for two reasons:

1. People like doing the things they are good at and familiar with, it may be rewarding to them, and their reaction can only be more negative if disinvestment is delayed. So often people talk about 'phasing out' something, then it gets forgotten about, and six months later it is still being done.
2. Most importantly, by stopping doing the unneeded things, much-needed time and space is created to introduce the new things.

KIDNEYS, SIR?
NO. PROSTATE...

Adoption and Diffusion Theory in PRODUCE

As leader you will need to have a strategy for ensuring that your vision/product is disseminated to the wider world. So in INVOLVE you will need to consider whether those you INVOLVE will also adopt and support the new ideas and practices that will be needed in PRODUCE.

Adoption Theory

We want to explore this in the context of leadership rather than simply product adoption, asking 'What is there to be learnt from this theory about how people adopt things that are new to them?' Rogers' diagram looks at different groups with respect to their acceptance of something new, whether it's the existence of the Higgs boson particle, or the electric car.

Roger's Innovation Adoption Curve

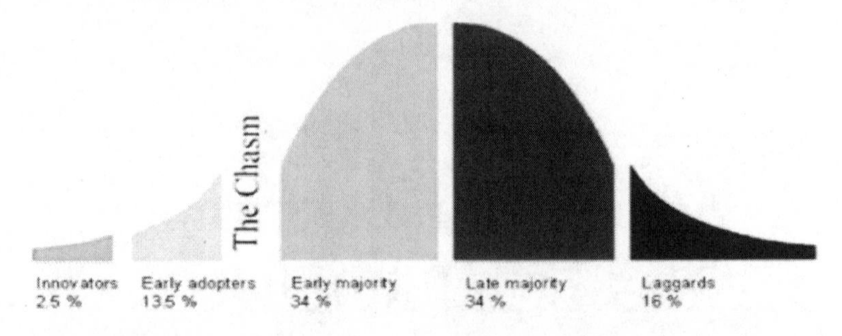

Trying to convince the mass of a new idea is *useless*.
Convince *innovators and early adopters* first.

Everett M. Rogers is widely known for the 'Innovation & Adoption' theory from research on how farmers adopted agricultural innovations (1957)

Innovators are well informed risk-takers prepared to try an idea or practice that is new to them: they represent 2.5%.

So as a leader, notice those around you who may take a risk with your VISION, get INVOLVED and use something new, without a whole host of evidence, in PRODUCE.

Early Adopters, often based on the positive response of Innovators, begin to use new methods. They are often informed people with educated opinion: they represent 13.5%.

So as a leader - ask who around you would adopt early, as they wouldn't want to 'miss out' on something new and would want to be in there early?

Early Majority are careful people who like to avoid risk, but will adopt the new ways of PRODUCE as soon as it has been proven to be useful by early adopters, relying on the recommendation of others who have experience: they represent 34%.

So as the Leader - who around you needs a bit more convincing and who will look to others for proof of success?

Late Majority – more sceptical are those who do not take up changes until it has become common place: they represent 34%

So as the leader, who around you in the workforce needs more convincing, and is only likely to adopt when a significant number of others do, or when they can see the bigger benefits? This might represent a willingness to adopt new working practices, within PRODUCE, when other people do.

Laggards – Those who avoid change (at all cost) and may not adopt the new methods at all or who will not, until the older alternatives are no longer available: they represent 16%

So as the leader – who is unlikely to change and even resist or openly oppose change? Would you be better off without them in your VIP process?

As the leader try thinking about your VISION as a product. We have used the word in a very broad context, as it could be a tangible thing or object, or it could be a service or concept or an idea, or just a new way of doing things. We hope VIP starts to give you some insight into how we might anticipate early adoption of your VISION, and the subsequent adoption of the methods and techniques your team will need to use in PRODUCE. There are some important things to note.

The type of adopter, from innovator through to laggard, is in no way a reflection of personality type, so avoid the 'Oh, they are always the laggard' comment. It is product-specific: think of this in your own context, which products do you like to be ahead of the game with, and which others don't you care for at all, maybe even dismiss or oppose – we all do it to various degrees?

Indeed it is easy to dismiss the laggard, and it is true you don't want to be wasting valuable time and energy on trying to convince them to adopt, when others may be chomping at the bit to do so. In any case, it will be others who ultimately persuade the late adopters and laggards to adopt, rather than yourself.

The biggest trap you may fall into is to ignore your laggards, even to dismiss what they are saying. DON'T, because, for any leader, swift adoption is often essential, and the aim of reducing adoption time should not be jeopardised by laggards, yet by ignoring them, there is a danger they could shout even louder, and slow down adoption. You may decide it is time to 'let them go', or assist them 'moving on', and this could be right for both parties. However, this may not be an option, and even if it is, consider this, the laggard could be a friend in disguise, whatever they are voicing in concern or opposition may well be shared by others and especially the late adopters, and as the laggards and the late adopters could add up to roughly half of those you have to engage in PRODUCE.

Also, the laggard may have some very valid points. OK, so they might express them in the wrong way, get angry, shout, send aggressive emails, and in turn you may wish to take them on, get into an argument with them, and tell them exactly what you think of them and their ideas. Be careful, you are entering 'the game' and remaining detached from the negative emotion, while acknowledging it, is the skill of a good leader. The challenge is to listen to them, distilling out any valid negatives, to leave the core message and then, by addressing the issues and concerns that are being pointed out, it will allow PRODUCE to proceed at greater pace.

'Yes I can see some benefit to this and I am moving closer to your way of thinking'

However, the focus should be to get the early adopters on board, as advocates of your VISION in order to PRODUCE effectively. Innovators could also play their part in promotion yet be careful as one feature of some innovators is that they move on to the next idea quickly or become too passionate about it, so that they almost belittle others for not being where they are.

There is then often a pause, a gap before the early majority latch on and adopt. This is highlighted in the diagram as a chasm (delay/time lapse) and can exist for many reasons including.

- Emotional attachment to what is already there, 'I like it this way, and I'm comfortable and familiar with it'.
- Price and ongoing cost, 'Can we afford this?'
- Other costs, 'Can I afford to be personally involved, and what is the impact and demand on me'
- Compatibility, or perceived lack of compatibility with other ways of doing things
- Lack of evidence, the long-term proof that it does what it says
- Just another change, 'Done something similar before and it didn't work'
- Choice confusion, there are several alternatives, so why not sit it out and see which proves more successful?
- Why this now, there will be something newer in a matter of months?
- Risk, the perceived consequences that may work against them, the risk that:
    - 'If it works too efficiently they will not need me any more'

- 'I won't be able to adapt to this new way, I'm too set in my ways'

- 'There is a risk to my reputation if this doesn't take off'

The leader would be off to a great start if they were able to identify the reasons the chasm between early adopter and early majority might exist and provide answers right up front for each of the reasons, in the attempt to reduce the impact of the chasm and decrease the time to adoption. The Diffusion Theory may help you understand how your team come to make their decisions.

Diffusion Theory in PRODUCE

Further work by Rogers (1995) went on to explore diffusion, the process by which innovation is communicated through channels over time and when decisions to adopt are not authoritative/instructed 'You will do . . . ' or collective agreements, 'We are all in agreement to do this', but when each member of the system faces their own personal decision as to whether to adopt.

This poses another question to the leader, 'Is it best to just tell people to do it?'. Well, maybe on occasions you should, or indeed need to, just give the instruction that a certain action or change is to happen. However, leadership is about inspiring not instructing, it is about enthusing those to follow the VISION wherever it originated: remember the 'ask' or 'tell' of Merrill and Reid?

There are five key steps in diffusion as defined by Rogers:

1. Knowledge – the person becomes aware of the innovation and has some idea of how it functions and its uses.
2. Persuasion – the person forms a favourable or unfavourable attitude towards the innovation
3. Decision – the person engages in those activities that lead to the choice as to whether to adopt or reject an innovation
4. Implementation – the person puts the innovation into use
5. Confirmation – the person evaluates the results of the innovation and the decision they made

Ask yourself as the leader, what is your part in helping people through the process of diffusion? What knowledge do people need, what persuasion techniques could you deploy (storytelling), what could help concrete a person's decision, what do they need to help them do it and how can you constantly evaluate and feedback the benefits?

The Change Curve in PRODUCE

If your VIP is within a 'start-up' company or team, you may have the luxury of hand-picking those who will support your VISION, be easy to INVOLVE and committed to PRODUCE. However, in most situations where VIP will be applied, there will be existing people who have been working in certain established ways with tasks they are familiar with. The change curve shown opposite gives some idea of the progression in 'think – feel – behave' that we all will go through when facing change.

The Change Curve is based on a model originally developed in the 1960s by Elisabeth Kubler-Ross to explain the grieving process. Since then it has been widely utilised as a method of helping people to understand their reactions to significant change or upheaval. Don't be tempted to underestimate the impact of change.

Kubler-Ross proposed that a terminally ill patient would progress through five stages of grief when informed of their illness. She further proposed that this model could be applied to any dramatic life-changing situation and, by the 1980s, the Change Curve was a firm fixture in change management circles. The curve, and its associated emotions, can be used to predict how performance is likely to be affected by the announcement and subsequent implementation of a significant change. You may find great change stimulating, exciting and necessary, others however might be intimidated or afraid of what you perceive to be minor change.

The Change Curve

Although this is no new theory, it is still amazing how many companies and organisations ignore this vital understanding that we have about human responses to change. Time and again we see organisations implementing change and placing focus on policy, procedures and new ways of working without consideration of the implications of the Change Curve for them. A little more emphasis on using the Change Curve intelligently and effectively could quicken any process in PRODUCE.

In each of these stages of the Change Curve, you will need to lead your team through their problems. This can be difficult, as different members of the team will be on different parts of the curve at different times.

Denial:

'This can't be happening' or 'This won't apply to me' are classic phrases in denial.

At this point, with people operating in their comfort zone, and not wanting to face change, they may try to keep your VIP proposals at arm's length, and deny that it is even happening. It is interesting to note the human reaction highlighted in each quadrant. In particular the 'fear' aspect; our observations would lead us to the conclusion that this is often undeclared fear. People who move through from denial to fear may anticipate that change could affect their work or status, and with this insight often become afraid to express their fear, in the belief that to do so could leave them more vulnerable. Therefore the declaration, 'I can't do what is being asked of us' often goes unsaid, maybe because they are fearful that in any workforce reconstruction, people unable to change may not be needed.

The leadership challenge in denial is one of providing clarity. If the change will definitely happen, then the sooner people are told, and the clarity with which they are told, is essential. It does happen that the weaker or less resourceful leader will attempt to placate people at this stage, or make the message more palatable by failing to deliver the message accurately.

Remember, difficult times don't need timid leaders, who deliver unclear, ambiguous messages that may leave people clutching at straws or selecting the parts of the message they want to hear.

- Tell people as much as you know, don't be lured into using information as power, your honest message now, as hard as it may be to hear, will lead to greater trust in the future.
- Reassure as much as is reasonable, while being intellectually honest.
- Explain the need for change and the facts that underpin this need for change.
- Explain any expected benefits that will follow from change.
- Do not get into long, drawn-out discussions, but do allow people time to absorb and take on board the key messages, and arrange a future time to talk through changes in detail.

Resistance

The 'You can't do this' or 'It's not fair and won't happen' phase comes next.

As people digest the information and reflect on what is going to change and how it might affect them, it is possible that anger may be projected towards the change. This presents a leadership challenge that requires a certain maturity of approach. It is very difficult for people to become angry at policy or corporate strategy; anger has to be directed somewhere as it is impossible to get angry at nothing. It is often likely that the anger will be directed at the leader, whether they are the originator of the change or not. This is a natural process and allowing people to be angry is important, as they need to express themselves in order to move on through the cycle of acceptance. Poor leadeship and poor management often spends too much energy trying to suppress or prevent the anger, so, allow it to be expressed.

- Realise that anger is a form of energy that can be channelled towards acceptance
- Create opportunities for people to express their anger in a safe, controlled environment
- Be strong and remember some of that anger could be coming your way. Resist reacting to personal accusations, which you may regret later

It is impossible to stay angry for ever, people will move on, but as they do so, they are likely to experience sadness, as they let go of 'what was', let go of the way they did things, the patterns they worked, and the people they worked with. As the leader, judging the sense of both the feelings of the individual and the workforce can be a real test of emotional intelligence. It is vital to understand the impact of change and, where possible, to support people through it.

Support could go from a minimal informal nod, smile or acknowledgement, right through to making available more structured time for people to talk through what they may perceive as a 'loss'. It is important to remember that your relief that something is changing because it was ineffective, wrong, and unproductive or whatever, could be to a huge loss to the other person, and allowing them to grieve is important in order to move on.

We believe that, by handling the resistance phase well, leaders can encourage movement towards willing rather than grudging acceptance.

Exploration:

Exploration is the 'If this is going to happen how could I influence it?', or 'There could be something in this' phase.

As people move through exploration, they start to accept, which is either because they just accept, even though reluctantly at first, or because they start to look at what is new and seek to find things in it that work for them. This is a productive time for the leader and an opportunity not to be missed as while in this phase, people start to open their eyes to what is new.

They may display relief for a number of reasons. Perhaps relieved that they are through the anger and upset of the resistance phase, relieved that things are starting to settle and that the future is looking clearer, relieved that, even though they may not have admitted it at the time, they knew change was needed and was inevitable, even that it was the right thing to do, and what they were resisting was the process of change rather than any principles.

Remember:

- There may be training and re-education needs.
- It should now be possible to explain the opportunities, the possible benefits to the individuals and to introduce options.
- It may be useful to illustrate this change, with examples and evidence.

As people start to show an interest in what is new, it provides a rich ground for the leader to steer, motivate and inspire.

Commitment:
This is the 'This is going to work', and 'We can be the best at this' phase.

Within their commitment to the change there are opportunities, yet it is important that the leader is ever present to ensure that the VISION is still being pursued, that they are still in INVOLVE, and that enthusiasm, or over-enthusiasm, does not lead to PRODUCE going off in unplanned or inappropriate directions.

- You can look to maximise the benefits of the change and start to look for other improvements
- You can lead the individuals and the team to greater satisfaction in PRODUCE
- You may be able to enhance their VISION, their wish to INVOLVE and their desire to PRODUCE even more, leading to greater innovation.
- You can aim to increase the efficiency within PRODUCE

Importantly in this phase, you can look to consolidate all that is good, ensuring you take time to support and develop, and in turn build up a resilience that prepares people for the next change that will come at some point.

Herein lie the complications of this model which present an additional challenge for the leader. In complex working environments, where there is a range of influencing factors, both internal and external to any organisation, different individuals will be at different points on the change curve.

It is also likely that, with multiple changes needed, some individuals will be inspired by some of the changes whilst angry at other aspects of the changes, and perhaps denying the next set of changes, which are still on the horizon.

Do not forget that the leader is not exempt from this process either, so it is important to recognise as the leader just where you are and the impact that may have on others.

Self-management and support is as important to the leader as to those they lead, so access to a mentor, coach, trusted friend and confidante are essential.

Change is constant and for the successful business it has to be, so mastering strategies to ride these constant reactions to change is a crucial leadership quality.

Leading Clever People in PRODUCE

WITHIN THE SPECTRUM OF INDIVIDUALS YOU NEED to help you achieve VIP, there may be groups that can potentially give you particular problems. Clever people can be challenging to lead and the leader must consider the possibility that there are those who are intellectual equals or who are even more clever than him or her.

Having clever people among those around you is exciting but also can be challenging. It may help to attempt to define 'clever', which we would think of as, quickness of intellect, skilfulness in a particular act, having mental agility or maybe those identified as experts.

Firstly, we have found it helpful to acknowledge that those around us may actually be cleverer than we are. In everyday life, in teaching sessions, one can see this, and it is something that school teachers in a highly academic school, or companies that rely on the work of specialists with expert skills, face every day.

Goffee and Jones (2007) looked at leading clever people. There are certain characteristics of clever people:

- They know their own worth and, as their knowledge is transferable, we need them.

  So it is important their worth is recognised.

- They will seek an organisation that supports them and will move elsewhere if they do not feel supported.

  There is an old adage, 'people leave bosses not organisations', so lead them well and support them.

- They tend to ignore company hierarchy and titles. However, they like to be close to their work and will covet the titles that relate to their cleverness, for example 'Dr' or 'Professor'.

  So acknowledge any title they have.

- They expect instant access to the boss and, if this is not available, they feel that the organisation does not value them.

  Plan that they have regular access to you, their leader. They want to be influential, so harness that, don't suppress it.

- They are well-connected outside the organisation, for example in academic circles, and this increases their value to you.

  Allow them time to look outward and reap their personal rewards: PRODUCE will benefit too.

- They will get bored if not allowed to flourish intellectually.

Give them responsibility for testing tasks that stimulate thought and debate.

- They are unlikely directly to acknowledge your leadership but, if they keep in contact, they think you are OK!

  Keep them in regular contact, and build trust through great rapport.

Therefore, when leading clever people, there are certain steps that you, as leader, can take. Make sure the environment allows them to achieve their full potential and where possible protect them from 'organisational rain':

- Look at the rules and politics of the company, and try to streamline any rules for simplicity
- Recognise and acknowledge the importance of their ideas
- Allow them room to experiment, even though this will mean that sometimes they fail
- Show them that you are competent to help them
- Show them that you have supplementary skills in the same field, or that you have complementary skills in the same field, for example handling the clients

Responsibility, Accountability and Authority

THE CONCEPTS OF RESPONSIBILITY AND ACCOUNTABILITY can at times be confusing and the leader often needs to enable other people to understand why they are different. We find the following the easiest way to look at this:

- **Responsibility** is about what a person has got to do and is therefore, at least in part, in the future. 'You are responsible for ensuring this happens' (future tense).

- **Accountability** is about having to make sure that something has been done to an identified specification – time, date, quality, standard etc, and therefore it is defined in the past. 'You will be accountable for ensuring this has happened' (past tense).

As a leader, you will have to hold both yourself and the members of your team to account, and can undertake that task effectively only if there is real clarity around responsibility.

As a general point, it is worth noticing that as one becomes more senior in the team/organisation, the level of accountability often rises and the level of direct responsibility falls. As you become less responsible for actually undertaking many tasks and doing things, your responsibility to do so can diminish as others take on that role. However, you will become more accountable for ensuring it is completed and as the leader you will be held to account for any consequences, both positive and negative.

When monitoring the progress of PRODUCE, it will be essential to be specific about who has responsibility to do what, and who you will hold to account for what, which, in turn, calls into question the area of authority.

- **Authority** – there are various definitions of authority, yet we would like to use this in the context of legitimacy, as it can help provide the bridge between responsibility and accountability. In order to hold someone to account it is important that authority has been delegated to them and they have the legitimate role to undertake decisions and subsequent actions.

Monitoring Progress in PRODUCE

In PRODUCE most leaders will set themselves a clear timetable for assessing the progress of the project. The diagram illustrates the principal aim in assessing progress, that is to define the gap between where we have got to and where we want to be.

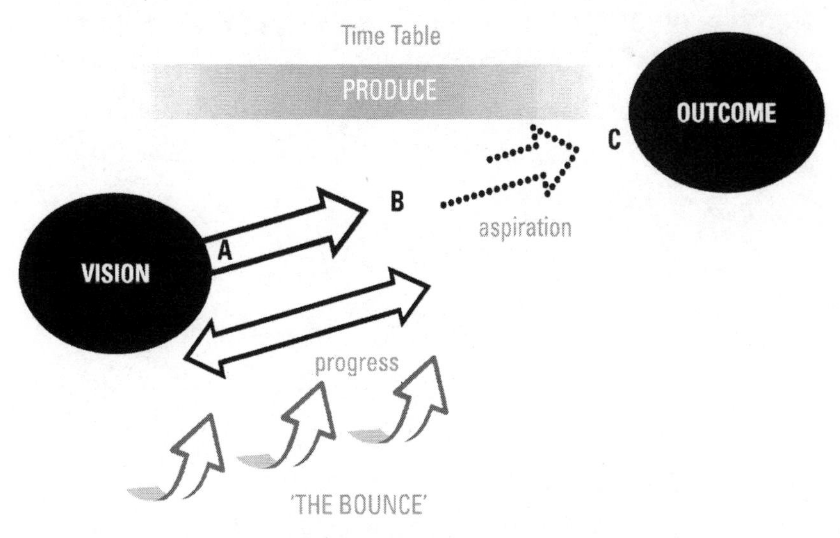

Without a clear plan, assessing progress can be difficult, but the following approach has worked for us, and helps to keep energy and momentum in the progress of PRODUCE

- First, talk about our success in getting from A to B

  As you move forward never forget to utilise the positive energy in acknowledging what you have achieved. Far too often focus is placed on what more you have to do and this constant assertion, especially in long-term goals, can be exhausting and demoralising for people. So it is important to remember that the only true measure of achievement is getting from A to B and that getting from B to C is still an aspiration. Constant re-assertion from the leader of what has been achieved is where the energy lies to provide for, what we call 'The Bounce', which will enable teams to find the energy to move forward and complete PRODUCE. So, ensure that the number of times you remind people of achievements far outweighs the number of times you tell people how far we still have to go, and remind them of the challenges ahead.

Then talk about how we get to our goal, C

- Is there something we can do better, allowing us to get from B to C more quickly and efficiently?
- Do we need to revisit VIP and see if VISION and INVOLVE need adjusting?
- Regularly assess responsibility and accountability

- Constantly remind people of the rewards at the end – what it will look like when achieved – how it will feel – and what they will hear others say.

Holding People to Account and Ensuring Performance in PRODUCE

MUCH IS SAID ABOUT PERFORMANCE MANAGEMENT, but it is often done too late, or when there is a sudden need for 'performance management' due to underperformance. If this is the case, the leader was accountable for seeing that one of the team was responsible for seeing that performance was assessed regularly. People fail for a reason and certainly don't usually set out to fail intentionally. So, why not:

- Return and revisit VISION and INVOLVE and PRODUCE, on a regular basis.
- What was the 'deal' in any case of difficulty?
  - Was it clear?
  - Was it sensible?
  - Was it realistic?

If the deal was OK:

- Seek an explanation for what was meant by acceptable performance, in this case
- Renew or gain commitment to the deal
- Which part of the deal did you give others permission to hold you to account on

If the deal is not OK:

- Define its deficiencies
- Redefine the deal
- Agree a new deal
- Agree to scrap the old deal

Maximising Personal Efficiency in PRODUCE

We hope that we have given you enough guidance, as the leader, to the VIP process. In PRODUCE, we have looked at both the 'engines' that will drive this part of the VIP process, and the 'brakes' which will try to slow it down and delay achieving your goal.

By clear and decisive, yet sensitive leadership, you will maximise your chances of achieving your objectives within the timescale you planned. Ensuring that you and your colleagues THINK and FEEL as you take ACTION, within PRODUCE is vital. Ensuring the health of your organisation by ensuring that the logical levels are in alignment will be important in helping you and your team to adjust and adapt to the inevitable changes that are necessary during your VIP process. The recognition and acceptance of the facets of people's behaviour, such as their own type of motivation, and their positions on the Change Curve, will allow all individuals in the team to fulfil their potential and feel their worth.

Part of the legacy of this VIP process will be the degree to which you have developed their own leadership potential, as well as how you have refined your own leadership skills

Success in the VIP process can never be guaranteed but we believe that good leaders will revisit the principles that we have described in the book. Many good leaders have a very high degree of intuition, as we have discussed, but none of us is perfect! Hence, awareness of leadership is likely to improve your performance as a leader.

However we haven't quite finished. You will want to see the result of PRODUCE becoming accepted

The VIP Process. When PRODUCE is Finished

When the VIP process is finished and you have succeeded, you are likely to want to gather the team together, for champagne and canapés, coffee and cake, or beer and sandwiches..

- Congratulations all round are in order!
- Debrief the team
    - It went well!
    - Despite our success have we lessons to learn for the future?
    - Could it have gone even better?
    - What did we as individuals, feel about our success?
    - Are there any general lessons for the future?

It may also be useful to reflect on the transaction or deals that we all entered into:

- All deals are transactions
- Transactions are two-way
- When we agreed to any deal
  - What did you / we get out of it?
  - Did we share the vision?
  - Did we feel involved?
  - Do we have a sense of achievement with the product?
  - Have we grown and developed as individuals?

The Future

What are we now planning to do with the product and what can we do to promote it?

We are not going to go into any detail as we feel this book is about leadership and not marketing! However, we would point out that Roger's adoption and diffusion theories will serve you well, as you seek to promote your achievements from VIP.

Good luck.

VIP Evaluation & Summary

Formal Evaluation of the VIP Process

GOOD ORGANISATIONS WILL ALSO WANT TO FORMALLY document the outcome of VIP.

Process

1. Time: Did the project come in on schedule?
2. Cost: Did the project come in according to budget?
3. Product: Did the project result in a product of acceptable quality and meet other product-related specifications?

Outcome

1. Use: Were the project's products/services used by its intended audience?
2. Learning: Did the project increase stakeholder knowledge and better prepare the organisation for future challenges?

3. Value: Did the project lead directly to the organisation's improved efficiency or effectiveness? Did the customer truly benefit as a result? What was the real return for the customer and company?

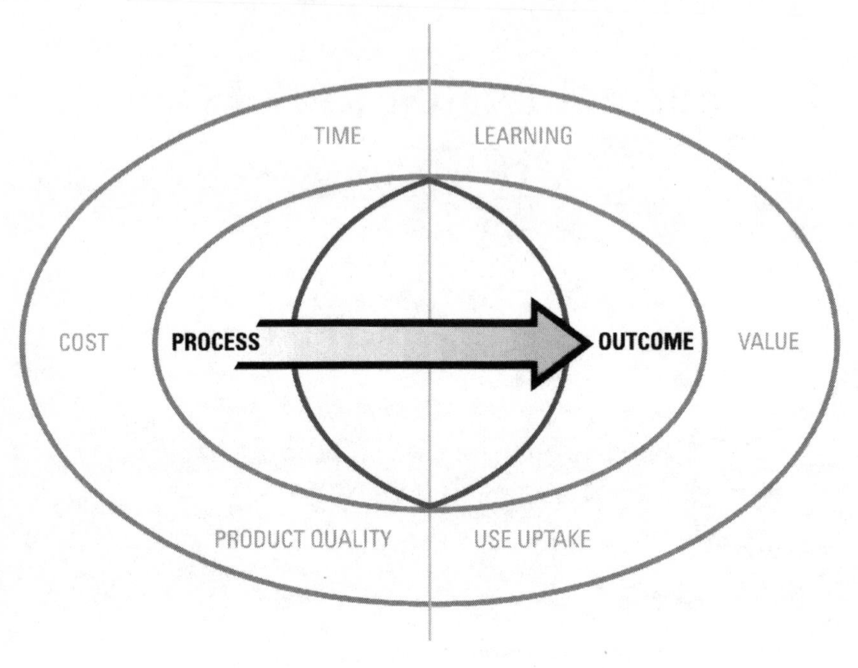

Summary

IN THIS BOOK WE HAVE TRIED TO EXPRESS OUR IDEAS concerning the VIP process and the importance we see in understanding ourselves and those around us, as a means of ensuring that the VIP process is successful. Despite writing the book and having thought about the issues at some length, transactional analysis reminds us continuously that it is difficult, perhaps impossible, to remain an adult and not to sometimes lapse back into either child or parent role. The most effective leaders are those who understand these dynamics and can match their role to the appropriate situation. In general, this will mean that they act in a mature, dependable way that attracts the respect of the team they lead.

Having completed this book, we feel we have used the VIP process effectively. We shared a VISION of the book you have read, for INVOLVE we asked Doug, Ron and Stephen who brought their own ideas to the project, and PRODUCE delivered the book.

* * * * *

We hope this journey through some important features of leadership have in some way helped you to refine your own VISION so that you can be even more able to INVOLVE those you need to help you PRODUCE and fulfil your dream. We hope that we have persuaded you of the wisdom of coming to know yourself better and to ask questions of yourself, and that we have introduced some new insights and entertained a little.

In VIP, the leader who listens allows others to contribute to VISION, to commit to INVOLVE, and to maximise their contribution to PRODUCE